Decorative Art in Modern Interiors 1973/74

Decorative Art in Modern Interiors 1973/4

yearbook of international decoration, volume 63, edited by Ella Moody Studio Vista Publishers, London

Glentanna designed by Adrianne Morag Ferguson for Heal Fabrics (and on page 99)

Acknowledgements
Decorative Art illustrates international
design in glass, ceramics, weaves,
printed textiles, paper and plastics, light
fittings and tableware, first produced in
the year preceding publication, with
recently designed houses and apartments.
Acknowledgements are due to all those
manufacturers and/or designers who
supplied photographs for publication
and to the following correspondents:
Dr Charlotte Blauensteiner of the
Österreichisches Institut für Formgebung
Vienna.
Frau Baumlehner of the
Landesgewerbeamt Baden-Württemberg,
Stuttgart.
Atushi Yoshinaga
of the Industrial Products Research Institute, Tokyo.
Enrichetta Ritter of Milan.

Published in London by Studio Vista Publishers
Blue Star House, Highgate Hill, N.19
and in New York by The Viking Press, Inc
625 Madison Avenue, New York, N.Y. 10022
ISBN 0 289 70344.1
U.S. SBN 670-26277-3
Library of Congress catalog card number 6-36913
Printed and bound in Great Britain
by Shenval Press Ltd, Harlow

CONTENTS

INTRODUCTION

The consumer is involved

How many thousands of designers in the world and why?

It has been suggested that the variously-styled craftsman/architect/designer exists in order to articulate the public's subconscious need. 'With today's anonymous society it has become essential for artists to provide for consumers the means by which to express themselves,' says glass designer Sam Herman, lately of the USA, now lecturing at the Royal College of Art, London. Anxious that young artists should not fail in their task for lack of facilities – 'students are too often suddenly pushed over the cliff without means of support' – Herman pioneered The Glass House where blowing and marketing can both be experienced and the consumer gets close to production.

It follows that whether or not the public believes it needs designers, the designer needs a public. How and what he is doing, of necessity, depends upon where he finds the public.

For the art college-trained glass designer, neither British nor American industry is looking. The furniture designer is faced by a technology for which he may be trained but with few openings. The ceramist can be, from the nature of his craft, independent and commercially viable.

In the opinion of Jack Lenor Larsen it is mainly in the textile field that the craftsman has made a significant contribution to industry. In America this has been due largely to the flair and genius of one woman – the late Dorothy Liebes.

The furniture designer may, like John Makepeace, make a path of his own.

Makepeace, living in the English countryside, sees furniture as 'some form of abstract sculpture, each object a blend of the designer's and craftsman's skill, which is further dictated by the choice of material: form, colour and texture are evoked by that choice. This interaction is subtly refined for specific commissions. The vital factors: an individual customer, a specific environment, the pressure or luxury of the budget: all refine or define the making of individual objects.'

It is, however, the ceramist, from his relative independence, who has developed – more accurately, retained – his position in the craftsman-designer situation.

Realistically, faculties in British colleges plan curricula with practical content but the ceramics course of Harrow School of Art ensures that every student can throw sixty decent cups in sixty minutes. This in no way conflicts with the need 'to make the student aware of the richness of life open to him as a creative craftsman'.

The college insists 'it is essential that intending students are convinced of the rightness of becoming potters. The bias of the course is towards individual work of high quality with stress on fine craftsmanship and professional standards. Although many production methods are taught, throwing is the cornerstone of the practical work. This is of utmost importance both as an ideal and a practical necessity.' The successful are fitted to set up and run their own workshops. Demand for hand-crafted ware is rising and work from a dozen workshops can be seen in Heal's London store, selling on the same floor as tableware from the big manufactories of Europe – Rosenthal, Wärtsila, Gustavsberg: its attraction, a subtlety only to be appreciated in the hand.

Output is surprisingly large from workshops rarely consisting of more than six people. Richard Batterham works alone, producing thousands of pieces from five or six firings a year. Shallow, flat, unglazed casseroles with ash or tenmoku-glazed interiors, jugs, crocks, bowls and teapots very much in the English domestic tradition are as characteristic of Batterham's output as are the cut-sided boxes and bowls and the individual bottles that look to China for their sources of inspiration.

'If you make what you like, you will find people who like it too' says Alan Caiger-Smith, confident that people will continue to like his lustre-glazed goblets and bowls.

The Craftsmen Potters Association's shop in London exhibits and sells the products of its 140 members, a sizeable proportion of British craftsmen and women, including the doyen of the ceramists, Bernard Leach. The shop is non-profit-making but functions successfully both as retail and wholesale outlet for work ranging from the humble ash-tray to massive sculptural jars, although not everything is strictly utilitarian. Stoneware predominates. The recently re-constituted British Crafts Centres also exhibit and sell but are grant-aided: furniture, jewellery, glass, prints, weaves and ceramics, including the sculptural and the experimental (for communicative art is on the increase) are shown. Neither the Craft Centres nor the Craftsmen's Shop are right on the path of the average shopper but their locations are known to those who appreciate an object made perfectly by hand and informed by the artist's spirit – and the craftsman often likes to know who it is who has bought his work. If this seems idyllic so – at a superficial glance – is the whole of the North European scene. The highly esteemed Scandinavian designer in glass, wood or textiles is surely in even closer rapport with his public ?

In the USA, news of craftsmen's shows can fill fourteen close-packed pages of *Craft Horizons,* a journal which itself exemplifies the vitality of the American crafts scene. Paul S. Donhauser, Professor of Art Ceramics at Oshkosh, Wisconsin, has outlined the diversity of the New Directions in ceramics which have developed from new freedoms in curricula since the 1950s.

'Potters are educated less as craftsmen than as artists, using clay as a convenient or expedient medium in which to give form to personal ideas and concepts. A great deal of very fine work is still being carried on in earthenware, stoneware and porcelain in traditional form-concepts, with the romanticism of reduction-fired stoneware of predominant interest.

'In contrast to this an entire body of work loosely identified as "bent ware" is being created. Some potters intend nothing more than a quiet, unassuming utilitarian vessel, while others strive to use the wheel-thrown shape as a departure. In the latter case, the pieces are therefore frequently paddled, dented, pinched, squeezed or otherwise changed in order to achieve asymmetrical contrasts. One aspect identifies with Abstract Expressionism. This is approached without necessarily any clear notion of what will be the end product and dramatic changes may occur while the piece is being constructed. An unfinished or incomplete appearance may result from the stress of making decisions while a piece is in progress. Size alone may be said to characterise one style, because large scale typifies America. Minimal and conceptual art also influence a body of ceramic sculpture: a variety of construction techniques can include slip casting, press-moulding, jigger-moulding, the use of blanks from industry, the inclusion of found objects and non-ceramic material.

'Within a broad range of what I shall call social commentary, a number of additional distinctions can be made. Easily recognised signs and symbols such as the gun or bullet, stars and stripes are integrated into forceful commentaries. In order to achieve heightened levels of expression, flamboyant colours and exaggerated proportions are often used. When a more universal satirizing is intended, a complex intermingling of stylised motifs is employed.'

These styles are typified on pages 148–9.

An enthusiast for the modern wave in America is Kimpei Nakamura, a young, brilliant Japanese ceramist: 'Lack of tradition in American ceramics spurred the creation of objects and a release of the latent passion contained in simple clay and fire. When this tendency is matched by today's demands and creative forces it gives rise to unbelievably free and fascinating work: when the same innate power loses direction there is danger of it deteriorating into playing with mud. Nevertheless, American potters produce work because they have "something to say": it belongs to, and can be understood only by, the younger generation. . . .'

But from these countries themselves comes criticism: from Sweden is a cry of despair from the glass designers no longer able to blow so freely under the forced 'rationalization' of Swedish glass industry. In Japan the essence of traditional pottery, it is said, can be mastered only by cultured men. Today, says Nakamura, 'it is too often characterised by meaningless formalization of a traditional style with superficial beautification'. Change is coming in the folk-craft pottery villages, forced to convert to making domestic tableware, even forced to put handles on cups to accommodate imported drinking habits, but there is no effort 'to bring ceramics into the main stream of contemporary culture, much less that of the young generation'.

The artist as a competent craftsman: the craftsman infused by the independent creative spirit of the artist: one man may wear both hats and his intent, both as craftsman and artist can come through loud and clear in a one-man exhibition. In other contexts it is often necessary to differentiate his roles.

Reaction to comprehensive exhibitions on local, national or international scale
make clear that failure of intent to distinguish between the two is an important basis
for adverse criticism.

From a critique of the New York State Craftsmen 1972 exhibition — an exhibition initially
organised in 'response to a growing public concern for the craftsman and his work in
society' there is the comment: 'As a spectacular of sophisticated craftsmanship the
exhibition was a success. In terms of relating crafts to the general public it was a
failure. . . . In pricing his objects as he must for a select clientele, the craftsman is no
longer functioning as did the traditional craftsman in supplying the needs of society.'[1]

The public needs the artist to give expression to its own needs but he is a still-
unfamiliar figure, divorced from his original utilitarian function. The public is made
uneasy if it is not helped to know what meaning and value it should give to his
creations by being present at the creation or initiated into the artist's secret.

In this respect The New Domestic Landscape created by Italy at the Museum of
Modern Art in summer, 1972 was a clear model of intent. No clay works on which
the message could be spelt out, literally, were included. Instead, forms fittingly
represented a country in which the engineer is in the highest stratum of artist-
craftsmen. Divided into two main sections, Objects and Environments, and several
sub-sections, the exhibition displayed:

'Objects selected for their form, judged upon aesthetic and technical criteria.'
'Objects whose formal characteristics are derived from or motivated by, the
semantic manipulation of established sociocultural meanings.'
'Objects which are flexible in function . . . and permit more informal patterns of
behaviour than those currently prevailing.'

Environments represented two, opposite, current attitudes to environmental design
in Italy: the first involving a commitment to design as a problem-solving activity:
the second, or counterdesign attitude, emphasizing the 'need for a renewal of
philosophical discourse and for social and political involvement as a way of bringing
about structural changes in society.'

The Objects represent the work of a decade during which Italy emerged as a dominant
force in design. The Environments represent a view of the future, on the one hand in
terms of today's technological possibilities, on the other as a demonstration by those
rendered unable to articulate their ideas in any material form, who instead channel
their energies into the staging of events and the issuing of polemical statements,
their approach thus paralleling that of many artists in other media who view art in
purely conceptual terms.'[2]

Need it be said that this exhibition too received adverse criticism? Criticism that the
artifacts are products not of craftsmen, because manual work is despised, but of
designers and architects forced into production — and limited-run production at
that — of modern objects for the rich. Perhaps the criticisms should be read as directed
to Society which produced the conditions, rather than to the organizers of the
Exhibition and individual designers. While they were not able to change the
environment they succeeded, marvellously one may think, in changing the shape
of some of its parts.

Many of the Objects in the Exhibition are to be seen in various issues of *Decorative
Art*. On the following pages are glimpses of the specially built Environments.

As for the Counter-design Movement, it is necessary to read Enzo Mari's essay
(as he did not give his ideas material form) or that of Ugo la Pietra who added some
sketches, or perhaps that of Superstudio which ends with 'a short moral tale on
design, which is disappearing'.

E.M.

[1] *Craft Horizons,* June 1972
[2] *Italy: the New Domestic Landscape* ed Emilio Ambasz
The Museum of Modern Art, New York: Centro Di, Florence

INTRODUCTION

Le Designer Aujourd'hui

Combien de milliers de designers y-a-t-il dans le monde et pourquoi ?
Il a été avancé que le créateur-de dénominations variées-artisan-architecte-designer
existe pour l'expression du subconscient du public. 'Avec la société anonyme
d'aujourd'hui il est devenu essentiel pour les artistes d'offrir au consommateur les
moyens de s'exprimer' dit le maître verrier Sam Herman, auparavant aux Etats Unis,
actuellement chargé de cours au Royal College of Art, Londres. Inquiet que les jeunes
artistes ne puissent réussir dans leur tâche par manque de facilités 'les étudiants ne
sont que trop souvent jetés à l'eau sans moyens de survivre' Herman a été à l'avant
garde de la 'Maison du Verre' où soufflerie et marché sont etudiés et le consommateur
est mis en relation avec la production. Il s'ensuit que le public croyant ou non qu'il a
besoin de designers, le designer a besoin d'un public. Le style et la qualité de son
oeuvre dépendent nécessairement de l'endroit où il trouve le public. Pour le verrier qui
a suivi un enseignement spécialisé ni l'industrie britannique ni l'industrie américaine ne
sont concernées. Le créateur de meubles est mis en face d'une technologie pour
laquelle il a peut-être reçu un enseignement mais sans grand potentiel. Le créateur en
textiles est relativement bien intégré dans l'industrie et rencontre de plus en plus de
succès en tant qu'artiste. Le céramiste peut, de par la nature de son art, être
indépendamment et commercialement viable.
De l'opinion de Jack Lenor Larsen c'est essentiellement dans le domaine du textile
que l'artisan américain a contribué de façon significative à l'industrie, tout
particulièrement grâce au flair et au génie d'une femme — Dorothy Liebes. Le créateur de
meubles peut, à l'instar de John Makepeace, créer sa propre place au soleil.
Makepeace, vivant dans l'Angleterre rurale, voit les meubles comme une certaine
forme de sculpture abstraite, chaque objet le produit du talent et de l'artiste et de
l'artisan, inspiré de surcroit par le choix des matériaux: forme, couleur et texture sont
suggérées par ce choix. Cette interaction est subtilement perfectionnée selon les
commandes spécifiques. Facteurs essentiels: un client particulier, un environnement
spécifique, la restriction ou la latitude du budget: tous ces éléments déterminent la
création d'objets individuels. Toutefois, c'est toujours le céramiste qui, grâce
à son indépendance relative a developpé — ou, plus exactement, maintenu sa
position d'artisan-créateur. Objectivement, les départements concernés des collèges
britanniques établissent des curricula d'ordre pratique mais au cours de céramique à
Harrow School of Art on est unique: ne faisant pas cas des diplomes, on rend possible
à chaque étudiant de produire soissante tasses acceptables en soissante minutes.
Ceci ne s'oppose en aucune façon avec la necessité de rendre l'étudiant conscient de la
richesse de la vie qui lui est ouverte comme artisan créatif. Le collège insiste 'qu'il est
essentiel que les étudiants potentiels soient convaincus de la valeur des potiers.
La tendance du cours est orientée vers le travail individuel de qualité avec accent sur
les standards artistiques et professionnels. Malgré l'enseignement de nombre de
méthodes de production, le tour d'un pot est la clef de voûte du travail pratique.
Ceci est d'une importance absolue tant idéalement que pratiquement.' Ceux qui
triomphent sont équipés pour installer et faire marcher leur propre atelier.
La demande pour des productions manuelles augmente et les oeuvres d'une douzaine
d'ateliers peuvent être vues chez Heal's, Londres, au même rayon que les services et
objets de table des grandes fabriques européennes: Rosenthal, Wärtsila, Gustavsberg.
Leur attraction est une subtilité qui ne peut être appreciée qu'au toucher. La production
d'ateliers comptant rarement plus de six artisans est étonnement grande. Richard
Batterham travaillant seul, produit des milliers de pieçs en cinq ou six cuissons par an.
Casseroles peu profondes, plates, non vernissées, à l'intérieur verni à la cendre ou au

tenmoku, pichets, pots, bols et théières dans un style domestique anglais très traditionnel sont aussi caractéristiques de la production de Batterham que les boîtes à pans coupés, les bols et les originales bouteilles qui ont été inspirés par la Chine.
'Si vous faites ce que vous aimez faire, vous trouverez des gens pour l'aimer aussi' dit Alan Caiger-Smith, confiant que le public continuera à aimer ses gobelets et ses bols glaçurés.
Le magasin de la Craftsmen Potters Association de Londres expose et vend les oeuvres de ses 140 membres, une proportion appréciable des artisans britanniques, hommes et femmes, y compris le doyen des céramistes, Bernard Leach. Le magasin est bénévole mais fonctionne de façon satisfaisante tant au détail qu'en gros pour des productions variant de l'humble cendrier aux massives jarres sculptées, bien que tout ne soit pas utilitaire. Le grès domine.
Les British Craft Centres exposent et vendent aussi mais reçoivent des subsides: meubles, bijouterie, verrerie, gravures, tissages et céramiques, sculpturales et expérimentales comprises (l'art de la communication allant croissant) y sont exposés.
Ni les Crafts Centres ni le Craftsmen Potters Shop ne sont exactement sur le chemin de l'acheteur moyen mais leurs emplacements sont connus de ceux qui apprécient un objet fait à la perfection à la main et inspiré à l'artiste – et l'artisan aime souvent savoir qui a acheté son travail. Si ceci semble idyllique ainsi en est-il – en aperçu superficiel – de l'ensemble de l'Europe du Nord. Le designer scandinave, tenu en grande estime, dans la verrerie, le bois ou le textile est certainement en rapports encore plus étroits avec son public.
Aux USA les annonces des expositions artisanales peuvent remplir 14 pages bien serrées de *Craft Horizons,* revue qui elle-même fournit une preuve de la vitalité de la scène américaine artisanale. Paul S. Donhauser, Professeur de céramique à Oshkosh, Wisconsin, a souligné la diversité des nouvelles orientations en céramique qui ont été engendrées par les nouvelles libertés dans les curricula depuis 1950.
'Les potiers sont moins éduqués en tant qu'artisans qu'en tant qu'artistes, utilisant la glaise comme un medium pratique ou rapide pour donner forme à des idées et des concepts personnels. Beaucoup de très jolies oeuvres sont encore réalisées en terre cuite, grès et porcelaine dans les concepts de forme traditionnels, avec le romantisme de la cuisson artisanale du grès. En contraste, tout un ensemble, vaguement qualifié de "déformé", se crée.
'Certains potiers ne conçoivent rien d'autre qu'un ustensile rassurant, d'une utilité sans prétention, tandis que d'autres s'escriment à n'utiliser la base tournée que comme point de départ. Dans le dernier cas, les articles sont, en conséquence, fréquemment: aplatis, dentelés, pincés, ressérrés, changés d'une manière ou de l'autre pour obtenir des contrastes asymétriques. Un style s'identifie à l'Expressionisme Abstrait. Ceci est abordé quelques fois sans notion claire de ce que sera le produit fini et des modifications substantielles peuvent survenir pendant l'élaboration de la pièce.
Une apparence de non fini, non complété peut résulter de la tension causée par les décisions à prendre en cours de fabrication. Seule la taille peut être assumée comme caractérisant un certain style, parce qu'une grande échelle est synonyme d'Amérique. Un art minimal et conceptuel influence aussi une certaine tendance de sculpture en céramique: une variété de techniques de fabrication peut englober la façon au tour, au moule ou au coulage, l'utilisation de flans industriels, l'inclusion d'objets trouvés et de matériaux non céramiques. 'A l'intérieur d'un vaste éventail de ce que j'appellerai commentaire social, un certain nombre de distinctions aditionnelles peuvent être faites. Des signes et des symboles aisément reconnaissables, tels que le fusil ou la balle, les étoiles et les rayures sont intégrés dans des commentaires frappants.
Afin d'obtenir des nivaux plus élevés d'expression, des couleurs flamboyantes et des proportions exagérées sont souvent utilisées. Quand on désire une satire plus universelle, un complexe mèlant des motifs stylisés est employé.'
Sur les pages 148/9 on trouvera quelques exemples caractéristiques de ce style.
Un enthousiaste de la nouvelle vague en Amérique est Kimpei Nakamura, un jeune et brillant céramiste japonais: 'Un manque de tradition en céramiques américaines a suscité la création d'objets et l'expression de la passion contenue dans la simple argile et le feu. Lorsque cette tendance rencontre les demandes et les forces créatives d'aujourd'hui elle conduit à une oeuvre incroyablement libre et fascinante: quand le même pouvoir perd son sens de direction, il risque de se détériorer en amusement avec de la boue. Néanmoins les potiers américains créent parce qu'ils ont "quelque chose à dire": cela appartient et ne peut être compris que par la jeune génération.'
Mais de ces pays eux mêmes vient une sévère critique: de Suède vient un cri de désespoir de la part des designers verriers qui ne peuvent plus souffler aussi librement à cause de la 'rationalisation' forcée de la verrerie suédoise. Au Japon, l'essence de la poterie traditionnelle, dit-on, ne peut être l'oeuvre que d'hommes cultivés.

'Aujourd'hui,' dit Nakamura, 'elle n'est que trop souvent caractérisée par la formalisation sans aucun sens d'un style traditionnel et d'un embellissement superficiel.'

Le changement se produit dans les villages de poterie artisanale, forcés de s'obliger à fabriquer des objets de table domestiques, forcés même de mettre des anses aux tasses afin de satisfaire les façons de boire importées; mais 'il n'y a aucun effort fait pour introduire le céramique dans le principal courant de la culture contemporaine, encore moins celle de la jeune génération.'

L'artiste artisan compétent: l'artisan inspiré par l'indépendance créative de l'artiste: un homme peut porter ses deux chapeaux et son message, comme artisan et comme artiste, peut sonner fort et clair dans une exposition de ses seules oeuvres.

Dans d'autres contextes il est souvent nécessaire de diversifier son rôle.

La réaction aux expositions diversifiées à l'échelle locale, nationale ou internationale est une base importante pour la critique de l'opposition.

Des USA et d'une critique de l'exposition New York State Craftsmen 1972 – exposition initialement organisé en réponse à une 'inquiétude publique croissante concernant l'artisan et son travail dans la société' – vient ce commentaire: 'En tant que preuve de l'artisanat sophistiqué cette exposition a été un succès. En termes d'oeuvres artisanales par rapport au public en général elle a été un échec. En établissant les prix de ses oeuvres pour une clientèle choisie, l'artisan cesse de fonctionner comme 'artisan traditionnel qui répond aux besoins de la société. [1]

Le public a besoin de l'artiste pour exprimer ses propres besoins mais il reste une entité, divorcée de sa fonction utilitaire originelle. Le public est gêné s'il n'est pas aidé à savoir quel sens et quelle valeur il doit donner aux créations en assistant à leur élaboration ou en étant initié au secret de l'artiste.

Sur ce point 'The New Domestic Landscape' créé par l'Italie au Museum of Modern Art de l'été 1972 était un modèle d'intention claire. Aucune oeuvre de glaise épelant, littéralement, le message, n'y figurait.

Par contre, des formes représentaient à propos un pays où l'ingénieur est au plus haut de l'échelon des artisans. Divisée en deux sections principales, Objets et Environnement, et plusieurs sous-sections, l'exposition montrait:

'Des Objets choisis pour leur forme, jugés sur des critères esthétiques et techniques.'

'Des Objets dont les caractéristiques essentielles étaient dérivées ou motivées par la manipulation sémantique de raisons socioculturelles.'

'Des Objets qui sont flexibles dans leur usage . . . et permettent un style de vie plus décontracté que ceux qui avaient force jusqu'à ce jour.'

Les Environnements représentaient deux attitudes courantes et opposées au design environnant d'Italie: la première comprenant une volonté de créer comme activité résolvant le problème, la seconde, ou contredesign, mettant l'accent sur le 'besoin de modifier le discours philosophique et se commettant socialement et politiquement afin d'entraîner des changements de structure de la société.'

Les Objets représentent l'oeuvre d'une décade pendant laquelle l'Italie tenait la tête du design. Les Environnement représentent une vue du futur, d'un côté en termes des possibilités technologiques d'aujourd'hui, de l'autre comme une démonstration de ceux qui ont été rendus incapables d'articuler leurs idées sous aucune forme matérielle et qui, alternativement, concentrent leurs énergies à façonner les évènements et à émettre des formules polémiques, leur approche s'appareillant ainsi à celle de nombreux artistes dans d'autres media qui ne voient l'art qu'en termes de pures concept.' [2]

Est-il nécessaire de dire que cette exposition a reçu elle aussi une critique sévère ? Critique que les artifacts ne sont pas les oeuvres d'artisans, parce que le travail manuel est tenu en mépris, mais de designers et d'architectes obligés à produire – et encore de façon limitée – des objets modernes pour les gens riches. Peut-être devrait on lire les critiques comme des attaques contre la société qui a produit les conditions, plutôt que contre les organisateurs de l'Exposition et les artistes individuels. S'ils ne pouvaient changer l'environnement, ils ont réussi, splendidement pourrait – on penser, à en modifier les formes de certains de ses éléments.

Plusieurs des Objets de l'Exposition peuvent être vus dans divers numéros de *Decorative Art.* Quelques aperçus des Environnements spécialement construits peuvent être vus sur les pages suivantes. Pour le mouvement du Contre-design il est nécessaire de lire l'essai d'Enzo Mari (puisqu'il n'a pas materialisé ses idées) ou celui d'Ugo la Pietra qui a produit quelques esquisses, ou peut-être encore celui de Superstudio qui se termine par une 'courte morale sur le design en voie de disparition'.

[1] *Craft Horizons,* Juin 1972
[2] *Italy: The New Domestic Landscape* ed Emilio Ambasz
The Museum of Modern Art, New York: Centro Di, Florence

EINLEITUNG

Der Designer heute

Wie viele Tausende von Designern mag es in der Welt geben und warum gibt es sie ?
Es gibt Stimmen, die dem im verschiedenen Stilen arbeitenden Kunsthandwerker,
Architekten oder Designer die Aufgabe zuschreiben, die unterbewußten Bedürfnisse
der Öffentlichkeit zum Ausdruck zu bringen. 'Mit der Anonymität der heutigen
Gesellschaft ist es für den Künstler bedeutend geworden, den Verbraucher mit
einem Mittel zum Selbstausdruck zu versehen' meint der Glas-Designer Sam
Herman, der bis vor kurzem noch in den USA lebte und nun am Royal College of
Art in London liest. Darum bemüht, daß junge Künstler nicht schon am Mangel von
Einrichtungen scheitern – Studenten werden zu häufig ohne Erwerbsmöglichkeit
'plötzlich ins Wasser gestoßen' – richtete Herman 'The Glass House' ein, wo
Glasblasen und Verkaufen erlernt werden können und der Verbraucher der
Produktion nahe gebracht wird.
Es kann gefolgert werden, ob die Öffentlichkeit glaubt oder nicht, den Designer zu
brauchen, daß der Designer die Öffentlichkeit braucht. Wie er sein Auskommen
findet und was er macht, hängt notwendigerweise davon ab, wo er die Öffentlichkeit
findet.
Weder die britische noch die amerikanische Industrie bemüht sich um den an der
Werkkunstschule ausgebildeten Glas-Designer. Der Möbelentwerfer steht einer
Technologie gegenüber, für die er ausgebildet sein mag; es gibt jedoch wenig
offene Stellen. Der Textil-Designer ist relativ gut in die Industrie eingegliedert und
in zunehmendem Maße als Künstler erfolgreich. Der Charakter seines Handwerks
ermöglicht es dem Keramiker unabhängig und kommerziell lebensfähig zu sein.
Jack Lenor Larsens Meinung nach ist es hauptsächlich auf dem Gebiete der Textilien
wo der amerikanische Kunsthandwerker der Industrie einen bedeutenden Beitrag
geliefert hat – zu einem großen Anteil aber auch nur durch das Flair und Genie einer
einzigen Frau, der nun verstorbenen Dorothy Liebes.
Dem Möbelentwerfer bietet sich die Möglichkeit, wie John Makepeace, seinen
eigenen Weg einzuschlagen. Makepeace, der in England auf dem Lande lebt,
betrachtet Möbel als 'eine Art von abstrakten Skulpturen'. Für ihn ist jeder Gegenstand
eine Verbindung von entwerferischen und handwerklichen Fähigkeiten, die im
übrigen durch die Wahl des Materials bestimmt wird: Form, Farbe und Struktur
fogen wiederum dieser Wahl des Materiales. Diese Wechselwirkung wird für den
jeweiligen Auftrag subtil ausgearbeitet. Die wichtigen Faktoren sind: ein
individueller Kunde, eine besondere Umgebung, finanzielle Beschränkung oder
Unabhängigkeit: sie alle verfeinern oder bestimmen die Anfertigung des individuellen
Objektes.
Bedingt durch seine relativ unabhängige Lage hat der Keramiker seine Position in
der Handwerker/Designer Situation entwickelt – oder genauer gesagt gehalten.
Realistischerweise planen Werkkunstschulen in England Lehrpläne mit praktischem
Inhalt – Die Harrow School of Art ist jedoch einzigartig: wenig Wert auf Zeugnisse
legend ist man hier bemüht, sicherzustellen, daß jeder Student in sechzig Minuten
sechzig ordentliche Tassen drehen kann. Das widerspricht in keiner Weise der
Notwendigkeit, 'den Studenten dazu zu bringen, sich bewußt zu werden, welche
Reichhaltigkeit des Lebens ihm als schöpferischem Kunsthandwerker offensteht'.
Das College besteht darauf, 'daß es wichtig ist, daß der Student von Anfang an
davon überzeugt ist, daß Töpfer zu werden, für ihn das Richtige ist. Der Schwerpunkt
der Ausbildung liegt auf der individuellen Arbeit von hoher Qualität mit besonderer
Betonung von sauberer Handwerksarbeit und beruflichen Niveau.
Obwohl viele Herstellungsmethoden gelehrt werden, bleibt das Drehen der

Eckpfeiler der praktischen Arbeit. Dies ist von äußerster Bedeutung – sowohl als Ideal als auch als praktische Notwendigkeit.' Die Erfolgreichen sind dann in der Lage, ihre eigenen Töpfereien einzurichten und weiterzuführen. Die Nachfrage nach Keramik- Handarbeit steigt ständig und man kann im Londoner Warenhaus Heal Arbeiten aus einem Dutzend Töpfereien sehen, wo sie in derselben Abteilung wie das Geschirr von den großen europäischen Manufakturen – Rosenthal, Wärtsila, Gustavsberg – verkauft werden. Der Ausstoß ist überraschend groß, bedenkt man, daß diese Töpfereien selten mehr als sechs Mitarbeiter haben. Richard Batterham arbeitet alleine; mit fünf oder sechs Brennungen im Jahr produziert er Tausende von Einzelstücken. Flache, niedrige unglasierte Kasserollen, innen mit einer grauen oder Tenmoku-Glasur versehen und Krüge, Töpfe, Schalen und Teekannen im traditionellen englischen Design sind ebenso charakteristisch für seine Arbeit, wie seine geradwändigen Dosen und Schalen und die eigentümlichen Flaschen, deren geistige Heimat China zu sein scheint.

'Wenn man das macht, was einem gefällt, wird man auch Käufer finden, denen dies ebenfalls gefällt' meint Alan Caiger-Smith, davon überzeugt, daß seine Kelche und Schalen in Hochglanz-Glasur auch weiterhin gefallen werden.

Der Laden der Craftsmen Potters Association (Vereinigung der Kunsthandwerk-Keramiker) in London besorgt die Austellung und den Verkauf der Produktion der 140 Mitglieder, ein beträchtlicher Teil der britischen Kunsthandwerker und -handwerkerinnen, zu denen auch der 'Doyen' der Keramiker, Bernard Leach gehört. Der Laden macht keinen Gewinn, erfüllt aber erfolgreich seine Aufgabe als Einzelhandels – und Großhandelsverkaufsstelle für Arbeiten, die von simplen Aschenbechern bis zu großen Skulpturgefäßen rangieren. Nicht alle Arbeiten sind unbedingt Gebrauchsgegenstände. Steingut steht im Vordergrund.

Ausstellungs-und Verkaufsmöglichkeiten bieten auch die kürzlich neu gegründeten British Crafts Centres, die jedoch subventioniert sind. Hier werden Möbel, Juwelen, Glas, Drucke, Gewebe und Keramik einschließlich skulpturaler und experimenteller Arbeiten gezeigt. Der Anteil der kommunikativen Kunst steigt. Weder die 'Craft Centres' noch der 'Craftsmen's' Laden liegen auf den Haupteinkaufsstraßen. Ihre Lage ist jedoch jenen bekannt, die einen Gegenstand zu schätzen wissen, der von Hand vollendet hergestellt und vom Geiste des Künstlers beseelt ist.

Der Künstler möchte oft auch gerne wissen, wer seine Arbeiten kauft.

Wenn dies idyllisch erscheint, so ist es – bei oberflächlicher Betrachtung – die Situation in Nordeuropa. Der hochangesehene skandinavische Designer von Glas, Holz oder Textilien ist sicherlich in einem noch engeren Kontakt mit seiner Öffentlichkeit?

In den Vereinigten Staaten können Nachrichten über Kunsthandwerker-Ausstellungen vierzehn engbedruckte Seiten von *Craft Horizons* füllen, einer Zeitschrift, die exemplarisch für die Vitalität der Situation des amerikanischen Kunsthandwerks ist.

Paul S. Donhauser, Professor of Ceramics in Oshkosh, Wisconsin, hat die Vielgestaltigkeit der neuen Richtungen in der Keramik, die sich durch eine neue Zwanglosigkeit in den Lehrplänen seit 1950 entwickelt hat, aufgezeichnet.

'Töpfer werden weniger als Handwerker als als Künstler ausgebildet. Sie verwenden Ton als nützliches und zweckmäßiges Medium, um eigenen Ideen und Konzepten Form zu geben. Eine große Anzahl von sehr guten Arbeiten wird noch in traditionellen Formkonzepten in Ton, Steingut und Porzellan ausgeführt, wobei die "Romantik" der Schmelz brennung von vorherrschendem Interesse ist.

'Im Gegensatz dazu wurde eine gesamte Arbeitsschule geschaffen, umfassend als "bent ware" bezeichnet. Einige Töpfer beabsichtigen nichts weiter als ausgewogene, schlichte Gebrauchsgefäße, während für andere die auf der Schreibe erstellte Form der Ausgangspunkt ist: die Arbeitsstücke werden deshalb oft beklopft, eingedrückt, zusammengedrückt oder in sonstiger Weise verändert, um asymmetrische Kontraste zu erzielen. Ein Aspekt ist mit abstraktem Expressionismus gleichzusetzen.

Diese Annäherung geschieht ohne notwendigerweise eine klare Vorstellung vom Endprodukt zu haben und umfassende Änderungen können vorkommen, während die Arbeit noch gestaltet wird. Ein unfertiger oder unvollständiger Eindruck kann aus dem Stress Entscheidungen zu treffen, während das Arbeitsstück im Werden ist, resultieren. Man kann sagen, daß die Größe allein schon einen Stil charakterisiert, da große Maßstäbe Amerika verkörpern. "Minimal Art" und "Conceptual Art" beeinflußen auch eine Schule der Keramik-Skulptur: die Vielzahl der Konstruktionstechniken können Hohlformguß, Pressformung, Schablonenformung, die Verwendung von Industrie formen und auch das Einschließen von beliebigen Gegenständen und nicht-keramischen Materialen umfassen.

'Im weitesten Sinne von dem was ich Sozialkommentar nennen möchte, können einige weitere Unterscheidungen gemacht werden. Leicht erkennbare Zeichen und

Symbole wie etwa Gewehr oder Kugel, oder Symbole des Sternenbanners werden zu kraftvollen Stellungnahmen vereinigt. Um größere Ausdruckskraft zu erzielen, werden oft leuchtend-grelle Farben und übertriebene Proportionen verwandt. Ist das Ziel mehr eine allgemeine Satire, so kommt ein kompliziertes Arrangement von stilisierten Motiven zur Anwendung.'

Die Beispiele auf den Seiten 148 und 149 sind typisch für diesen Stil.

Kimpei Nakamura, ein junger hervorragender japanischer Keramiker, ist begeistert von der modernen Bewegung in Amerika: 'der Mangel von Tradition in der amerikanischen Keramik spornte die Schöpfung dieser Arbeiten an – eine Freisetzung von schlummernder Leidenschaft, ausgedrückt in einfachem Ton. Wenn diese Tendenz den heutigen Ansprüchen und schöpferischen Kräften angepaßt wird, so kann sie unglaublich freie und faszinierende Arbeiten hervorbringen; wenn jedoch dieselbe angeborene Kraft sich verzettelt, so besteht die Gefahr, daß Ganze zu ''einem Spielen mit Lehm'' absinkt. Nichtsdestoweniger stellen die amerikanischen Töpfer ihre Arbeiten her, weil sie ''etwas zu sagen haben'': ihre Arbeit gehört der jüngeren Generation und kann auch nur von ihr verstanden werden.'

Aber selbst aus diesen Ländern kommt harte Kritik: aus Schweden der Verzweiflungsschrei der Glas-Designer, sie könnten unter der erzwungenen 'Rationalisierung' der schwedischen Glasindustrie nicht mehr so freizügig arbeiten. Man sagt in Japan, daß das Wesen der traditionellen Töpferei nur von gebildeten Menschen verstanden werden kann. 'Heute', sagt Nakamura, 'wird das allzu oft durch eine bedeutungslose Formalisierung eines traditionellen Stils mit oberflächlichen Verschönerungen gekennzeichnet'. Die Zeiten haben sich auch in den Dörfern der volkstümlichen Töpfer geändert. Genötigt sich auf Haushaltsgeschirr umzustellen, ist man jetzt sogar gezwungen Tassen mit Henkeln zu versehen, um fremden Trinkgebräuchen entgegenzukommen. 'Es gibt jedoch keine Bemühungen, die Keramik in das Bewußtsein der zeitgenossischen Kultur, viel weniger noch in das der jungen Generation zu bringen.'

Der Künstler als fähiger Handwerker – der Handwerker erfüllt mit dem schöpferischen Geiste des Künstlers. Beide Rollen können von einem Mann gespielt werden und seine Absichten, sowohl als Handwerker als auch als Künstler können in einer Einzelausstellung zum Ausdruck gebracht werden. In anderen Zusammenhängen ist es oft notwendig zu differenzieren.

Reaktionen zu umfassenden Ausstellungen auf lokaler, nationaler oder internationaler Ebene zeigen deutlich, daß ein Unterlassen zwischen den beiden Faktoren zu differenzieren ein Hauptgrund für nachteilige Kritik ist.

Die 'New York State Craftsmen 1972' – Ausstellung, ursprünglich ausgerichtet, 'um dem wachsenden öffentlichen Interesse am Kunsthandwerker und seiner Arbeit in der Gesellschaft Rechnung zu tragen', brachte diese Kritik aus den USA: 'Als Schau hochentwickelter Handwerkskunst war die Ausstellung ein Erfolg, sie war ein Mißerfolg insofern, daß es ihr nicht gelang, das Kunsthandwerk der Öffentlichkeit nahezubringen. Da der Kunsthandwerker die Preise für seine Arbeiten für eine ausgewählte Kundschaft festsetzen muß, hat er nun eine andere Funktion als der traditionelle Handwerker, der die Bedürfnisse der Gesellschaft befriedigte.'[1]

Die Öffentlichkeit braucht den Künstler, um ihren Bedürfnissen Ausdruck zu geben. Losgelöst von seiner ursprünglich 'nützlichen' Funktion ist er jedoch noch eine zu ungewohnte Erscheinung. Die Öffentlichkeit, die nicht weiß, welche Bedeutung und welchen Wert sie seinen Arbeiten beimessen soll, wird sich unsicher fühlen, wenn ihr nicht dabei geholfen wird, indem sie etwa bei der Schaffung der Objekte dabei sein kann oder vom Künstler in seine Ideenwelt eingeführt wird.

In diesem Sinne war 'New Domestic Landscape' von Italien im Sommer 1972 im Museum of Modern Art New York ausgerichtet ein Modell für eine klare Konzeption. Keine keramische Arbeit auf der – wörtlich genommen – ein Anliegen vorgebracht werden konnte, wurde aufgenommen. Statt dessen nahm man Formen, die passenderweise ein Land repräsentierten in dem der Ingenieur in der höchsten Schicht der Künstler/Kunsthandwerker steht.

Aufgeteilt in zwei Hauptabteilungen: Objekte und Milieus mit mehreren Unterabteilungen wurden auf der einen Seite Objekte ausgestellt, die nach ihrer Form ausgewählt worden waren und nach ästhetischen und technischen Kriterien beurteilt wurden.

'Objekte deren formelle Charakteristiken durch semantische Manipulation von etablierten soziokulturellen Bedeutungen abstammen oder motiviert werden.'

'Objekte, die in ihrer Funktion flexibel sind und deshalb ungezwungenere Verhaltensmuster gestatten als die heute vorherrschenden.'

[1] *Craft Horizons,* June 1972

Die Milieu-Abteilung zeigte zwei entgegengesetzte Anschauungen über Milieu-Design: die erste, die im Design auch eine Verpflichtung zum Lösen von Problemen sieht und die zweite oder 'Counter-Design' Anschauung, die die Notwendigkeit für eine Erneuerung der philosophischen Erörterung und des sozialen und politischen Engagement als Mittel für eine strukturelle Veränderung der Gesellschaft, betont.'

Die Objekte repräsentierten die Arbeit eines Jahrzehnts, im Verlaufe dessen sich Italien als führende Kraft auf dem Gebiete des Designs entwickelte. Die Milieus repräsentierten einen Blick in die Zukunft: auf der einen Seite im Hinblick auf die Möglichkeiten der heutigen Technologie auf der anderen Seite als Demonstration derer, die verhindert sind, ihre Ideen in irgendeiner materiellen Form zu artikulieren, aber statt dessen ihre Energie für das Aufziehen von Veranstaltungen und der Herausgabe von polemischen Erklärungen verwenden. Eine Auffassung, die von vielen Künstlern in anderen Medien geteilt wird, die Kunst rein begrifflich betrachten. Ist es verwunderlich, daß auch diese Ausstellung nachteilige Kritik erhielt ?

Kritik, daß die Objekte nicht von Kunsthandwerkern hergestellt worden sind, weil Handarbeit verachtet wird, sondern von Designern und Architekten, die in die Produktion gezwungen worden sind. In die Produktion von diesen – in begrenzter Anzahl hergestellten – modernen Objekten für die Reichen. Vielleicht sollte diese Kritik nicht an die Organisatoren der Ausstellung sondern an die Gesellschaft gerichtet werden, die die Bedingungen dafür geschaffen hat.

Eine große Anzahl der Objekte dieser Ausstellungen werden in verschiedenen Ausgaben von *Decorative Art* zu sehen sein. Auf den folgenden Seiten geben wir einen kurzen Einblick in die speziell eingericheteten Milieus. Für einen Überblick über die 'Counter-Design'[2] Bewegung sollte man Enzo Maris Essay (er gab seinen Ideen keine materielle Form) lesen oder den von Ugo la Pietra, der einige Skizzen beigefügt hat; vielleicht auch den Aufsatz von Superstudio, der mit 'einer kurzen moralischen Fabel über das Design, das im Aussterben begriffen ist' abschließt.

[2] *Italy: the New Domestic Landscape* hrsg. Emilio Ambasz
Museum of Modern Art, New York: Centro Di, Florenz

System of three different elements, of which one is linear and two angular. By arranging them differently, they can create areas with the following uses: bed, cupboard, bookcase (either longitudinal or free standing), shelves, seats:
fibre glass, rubber joints, cages of structural metal.
Extendible table with modular service units: a plain surface, a storage surface: steel structure with ABS plastic facing.
Chair, a corrugated form : fibre glass or rigid polyurethane.
Lamp, eight rotating elements: metal.
The predominant object of the design is made up of elements so composed as always to make their original purpose evident, while at the same time remaining open to a determination of their future purposes.
Designed by Gae Aulenti
Patrons: ANIC-Lanerossi: Kartell
Producers: Kartell assisted by Zanotta

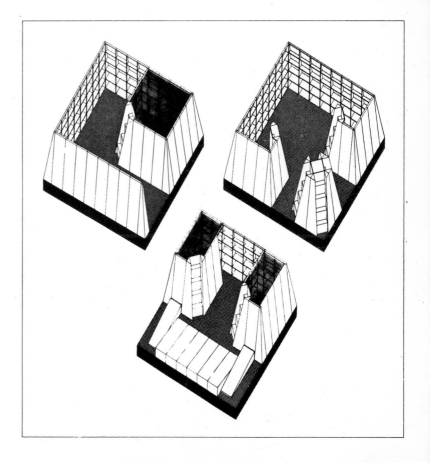

Project finalised posthumously, but very much in the line of development followed by Colombo from 1962 onwards. His researches in ecology and ergonomics led him increasingly to view the individual habitat as a microcosm, which should serve as the point of departure for a macrocosm attainable in the future by means of coordinated structures created through programmed systems of production.
Designed by Joe Colombo in collaboration with Ignazia Favata
Patrons: ANIC-Lanerossi
Producers: Elco-F I A R M, Boffi, Ideal-Standard, with the assistance of Sormani

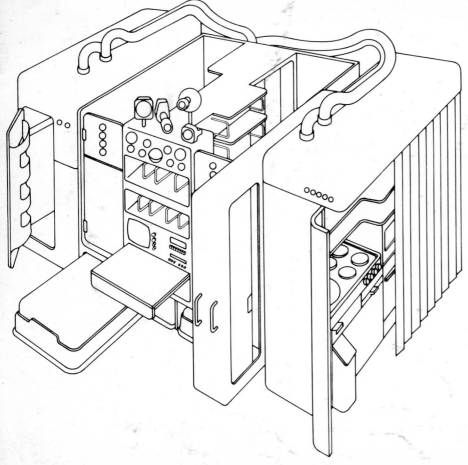

NIGHT

BREAKFAST

LIVING

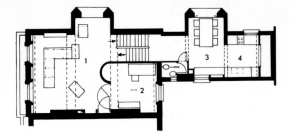

first floor
1, living room with stairs
 up from lower flat and
 to second/third floors
2, study
3, dining room
4, kitchen

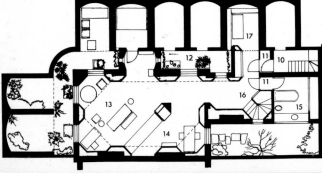

ground floor
5, entrance and stairs to lower floor
6, entrance and stairs to
 floors 1–3
7, studio
8, bathroom
9, bedrooms

basement
10, area and steps from street
11, lobbies
12, garden and vaults' series
13, living room
14, dining-kitchen
15, bathroom
16, stairs to ground floor
17, bedroom

and on pages 24/7

A substantial but no-longer-solid house typical of many in Pimlico, has been rescued, buttressed and internally restructured so that its spaces correspond hardly at all with the original plan. Only the vaulted cellars under the pavement are recognisable in the arcadian garden. No less than eight of these coal cellars opened into the area — a moat-like area — between street and house — on which lower level the lower orders used to enter.

The upper floors — first, second, third — were developed into a large family home for Roy Stout, his wife and four children. The first floor is given over to a large freely planned living area (on this page). This opens onto one balcony at the front of the house and to another larger one opening off the half level of the staircase above the main living area.

The small study/workroom at first floor can be shut off from the living area by folding doors or left open as a visual extension of that space. The kitchen and dining area (opposite) are on the half level below but at this point the rooms are open to the staircase so that from the front of the living room it is possible to appreciate the full depth of the house on the two adjacent split levels.

Two Maisonettes, Pimlico, London
architects Roy Stout and Patrick Litchfield

The lower maisonette is lived in by Pat Litchfield and contains two bedrooms, bathroom and studio on the ground floor. The main living area is in the basement — once dank and uninhabitable but now with more, and full-height, windows. It is entered by a semi-octagonal spiral staircase which prepares one for the 45° angle planning of the space, basically one big room containing a kitchen area but making use of the linked vaults as additional spaces and gardens.
The low slatted ceiling emphasises the horizontal distances and defines the main volume of the room.
The walls have been damp-proofed by building a thin inner skin wall leaving a varying sized cavity, producing facetted walls or columns rising clear above the edge of the slatted ceiling. This undulating wall creates a series of alcoves off the main

from pages 22/3

space and it is very difficult to determine
the exact limit of the enclosure — a feeling
emphasised by the removal of the wall
which originally separated the vaults from
the area.

The vaults thus exposed have become an
arcadian garden and especially when lit at
night their back walls seem to be the real
enclosure of the living room, below and
on next pages.

A sense of spaciousness and continuity
has been achieved throughout the house
by the consistent use of few materials.
Thus all the walls are white, curtains are
off-white linen, lowered ceilings which are
used to unite spaces which would otherwise
be split up by beams or changes of level
are a light olive green.

All upper floors are carpeted in a dark
khaki haircord; the basement has
heather-brown quarry tiles.

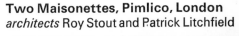

Two Maisonettes, Pimlico, London
architects Roy Stout and Patrick Litchfield

Dimmer-controlled fluorescent lighting is
generally concealed in troughs which
incorporate the curtain track, or in the
edges of the lowered ceilings.
Additional, tungsten, lighting is also
dimmer-controlled.

photo key

1, upper maisonette living area
2, the end-of-terrace house,
   Pimlico, London
3, upper maisonette kitchen and dining
   area
4, lower maisonette living area
5, night view of the vaulted garden
6, living area from the lower kitchen
   counter
7, bedroom set into one of the vaults
   accessible from the main living space
8, *overleaf* night view of the living area
   from the arcaded garden
on book wrapper the dining alcove set
into one of the vaults

4 5 6
  7   *photographs* Richard Einzig

see pages 22/5

floor plan
1, living room
2, dining room
3, kitchen
4, parents' bedroom
5, children's bedroom
6, breakfast bar
7, bathroom
8, entrance
9, veranda
10, closed court
11, storage (reservation for a sauna)

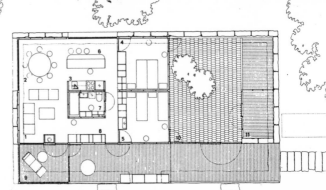

Holiday House at Råmüs, Siuntio, Finland
architect Juhani Pallasmaa

For summer sun and winter snow, this holiday home is near to one of the thousands of lakes which shimmer in the Finnish landscape.
Existing stone foundations of a former cow-shed together with its concrete floor, dictated the form of the rectangular plan of the house with its closed court.
To achieve close contact to the terrain the house was in fact set lower, inside the stone foundations which now form a U-shaped wall, two metres high, cutting into the slope on which the house is located and opening to the view over the fields and lake.
The simple all-wooden construction was therefore placed directly on the original concrete floor. The common spaces and bedrooms are around a bathroom/kitchen core, the bedrooms opening also to the interior court.
Inner walls, ceilings and doors are all of white stained pine, floors and windows of the same wood stained grey and brown respectively.
A terrace, partially covered and closed, runs the whole length of the building, facing south.

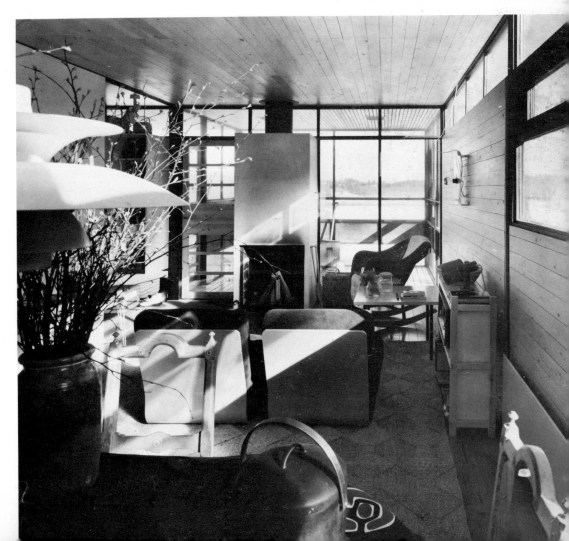

photographs Richard Einzig

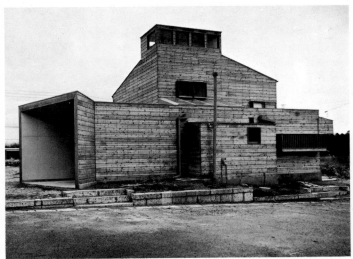

The Fu Residence, Japan
architect Kisaburo Kawakami

1 2 4
3

A Yellow Submarine of a house, floating calmly
where it finds itself.
The spirit with which the architect sought to
imbue it is expressed in some lines:

Glass Tower
A mass of houses this beautiful landscape
will one day be.
On a small part of it stands my glass tower.
Inside the glass tower there is no direction.
Light, wind, and blue sky are together in private space.
It becomes the house of the moon and light.
Stand still for a while.
The white wall expands and contracts with light.
Corners disappear.
The front elevation becomes a plan.
and the plan hangs in the air.
Then geometry disappears.

Breathing
The house breathes.
Hard shell and soft spaces.
You feel the breath of the house in these spaces.
The house holds the wind and sun.
Then flies high in the sky with evidence of the earth.
When darkness dominates the world,
a streak of light breaks the darkness, and frees the earth
This is a lighthouse in the night sea.
A streak of light in the morning mist,
flows inside from without, and rushes out from within.
The King, called the Sun has just arrived.
The light fuses together with different direction
and amount.
From white to yellow, yellow to red.

The wall and the long tube.
The wall prevents a private space.
The wall opens itself to society.
A house is where men get together,
and walls get together. . . .
I want to walk there!

and on pages 32/

from pages 30/1

In and out, front and back, disappear.
Soon the wall changes to the tube. . . .
The long tube is the evidence of order.
The free expansion of light and wind.
Facilities which support the house. . . .
Locus of three: Man, Things, Nature.

Moving
It moves when you operate an image.
It easily moves here and there
into the sea, cloud, forest and desert.
Children, young man and a woman on board.
Lights appear one by one in the silhouette of the mass.
It breathes and floats by taking the length
and breadth of man's locus.
Suddenly, this mass might disappear.
Where are they going to sail ?
Where ?

The Fu Residence, Japan
architect Kisaburo Kawakami

Yellow Submarine
Beatles. They sing.
I kept seeking for the place with traces of their songs.
I looked for the street which leads the children to heaven.
It was on the stairs.
I looked for blue sky, gentle breeze, green
sea in the big glass.
I looked for the sun on the white wall.
In the yellow world,
Pepperland and Yellow Submarine.
Yes, the Yellow Submarine with the group
of Sergeant Pepper's Lonely Hearts Club Band on board.

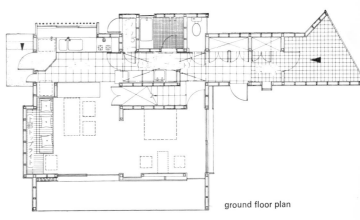

ground floor plan

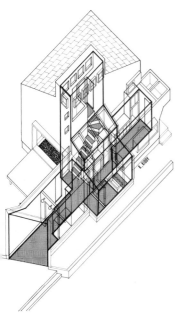

1, south entrance
2, north-east side view
3, entrance with toilet room
4, east side view
5, dining area of sitting room
6, tatami room
7, staircase

5 6
7

photographs Tohru Waki
courtesy Kenchiku Bunka

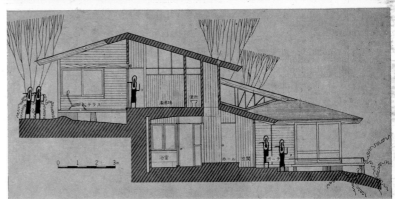

The In Residence, Japan
architect Hatsue Yamada

The architect wanted to leave Nature as
beautiful as it is.
Soon there will be other houses on the
slopes of the still-wooded hill where this
one is built.
How many can live in the wood and
still be 'alone with Nature'?
It is a house for a family of
eight. the oldest member of
which is 88, the youngest 22.
For each individual the house provides an
environment in which to be 'alone' and for
each as member of a group an
environment in which to be 'together'.
Thus each generation group has its own
level or its own terrace for its different way
of life.

The sitting, or family, room is a contact
point at which individuals unite.
Combined in it are the functions of eating
and tea-ceremony in the tatami-mat space.
The house is on the eastern slope of the
hill and is designed in such a way that
each room has equal benefits of sunshine
and breeze and each an individuality to
harmonise with its aspect.

1, east side deck
2, bedroom
3, west side
4, terrace
5, 7, living room
6. living room from entrance hall

and on pages 36/7

from pages 34/5

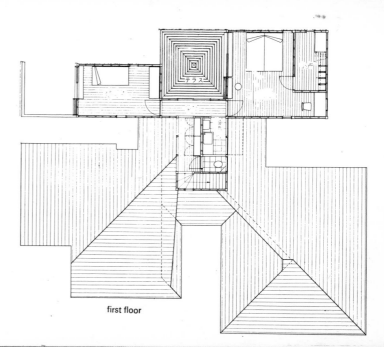

first floor

The In Residence, Japan
architect Hatsue Yamada

photographs Sam Sawdon

The possible arrangements of four rooms within a rectangle are limited. Hence the basic similarity of so many urban apartments and the challenge to the occupier to stamp upon one of them his individuality.

The owner of this apartment is a collector of 'twenties and 'thirties furniture and decoration: it happens that the compact, modern block in which it is situated reflects in its functional, corrugated-iron cladding more than a touch of the same period.

Wall surfaces are important to Chiu too: entrance and hallway as well as end- and window-walls of the living room are treated with soft flannel-grey Flotex: at the opposite end of the textural and reflective scale is the wall lined entirely with mirror-mosaic.

Endlessly pictured in it are the trees and the sun and the night sky as well as the chairs made by Breuer at the Bauhaus, the rug designed by Chermayeff during his period in London, the lamps and knick-knacks which echo the age of which Garbo, Crawford, Swanson and Dietrich were sex symbols.

Lines, angles and arcs of geometry are on or in everything; porcelain containers are cast as shoes, armchairs, automobiles; a Charleston-ing pair express the ideal of their time. Yet in this 1970s apartment, the 1930 scene composes wonderfully. From the kitchen it can be viewed, literally, through the two-way circular mirror which opens as a serving-hatch. The hallway turns into a clothes-closet – lined way to the blue bedroom and a study at the further end.

The whole apartment is unified with natural wool carpeting.

and on pages 40/1

from pages 38/9

Apartment at Regents Park, London
interior designer Chiu

Stephenson Mews, Dublin
architect Sam Stephenson

Tall timber doors screen the courtyard of this town house in Dublin the home of the architect and his family.

The small two-mews property was considerably re-structured. At ground level the brick wall was replaced by glass to provide a light and bright entrance hall: an opening to the right in the party wall between the two houses leads to the master bedroom at the front and to the living room at the rear. The unconventional reversal of living space has resulted in the quiet walled-in ground floor being used — apart from the living room — for sleeping accommodation. This spacious living room at the back of the house has a sunken, tiled-in conversation pit upholstered in black glove leather; the ceiling is of bleached Oregon pine.

Three steps on either side of the free standing brick fireplace lead to the gallery running the full height of the house.

Three long narrow windows here look on to the small rear garden and provide additional light for the dining room at first floor level, reached by another flight of stairs.

The link between the two houses at this level is the kitchen formed by an opening in the party wall. At one side, this connects with the family living quarters, and at the other with the main dining room, and study off it. A full-length window from the dining room leads on to the roof garden: it is also accessible by stairway from the entrance courtyard.

The design, with its many changes of level, results in a spectacular feeling of space. Colours are subdued, with deep tones used primarily to define the design elements.

The architect's week-end and holiday home on the borders of Wexford and Wicklow is illustrated overleaf

photographs Snoek Westwood and Norman McGrath

Among gently rolling hills overlooking the Slaney River this small Georgian farmhouse had been adapted, in the words of the architect, 'with rare insensitivity' during the Victorian era. However, because of its size and general plan Mr Stephenson found few problems in adapting it for his own family as a holiday home.

The entrance hall and main living room flooring is of old pine boarding which has been sealed and sanded and is partially covered with white, long-haired V'soske Joyce rugs. The living room which had retained its original Georgian windows, is decorated entirely in white, with the exception of the existing black marble fireplace. Designed by the architect, the four-piece seating unit is upholstered in white glove leather: its form accommodates a layoff area around the back providing space for ashtrays, books, drinks, etc. Lighting is by silver Rotaflex downlighters. Curtaining was felt to be unnecessary, as complete privacy is afforded by the site itself.

Over the fireplace hangs a piece of French kinetic art and on the opposite wall is a large eighteenth-century Indian temple hanging. The fireplace, with its old wheel-operated wind machine still in working order, has been given a new hearth of unpolished Wicklow granite.

An up-to-date kitchen was built into the former butler's pantry adjacent to the dining room — the dining room having been created from the over-large entrance hall from which it is now screened, left.

Existing white timber panelling in this part of the house was made good and the old fireplace removed and made good with similar panelling. The floor, which was also sanded and sealed, is partially covered by a red, long-haired rug. Specially designed dining chairs and table are of straight grained pine, lacquered red and upholstered in purple Irish tweed from Gaeltarra Eireann.

The house provides ample space for the architect's four children and the families of week-end visitors. As well as a games' room in a semi-basement there is accommodation for ten children, if need be, with their own bathroom and own approach staircase, at the rear of the house on the first floor.

photographs Norman McGrath

Ballynoe House, County Carlow
architect Sam Stephenson

text overleaf

The Washington home of the architect
architect Hugh Newell Jacobsen

The Georgetown district of Washington dates from the very early 1800s and its buildings are subject to a preservation order: remodelling and additions must not be visible from the street.

This is an 1803 house with 1840 additions but remodelled and with further additions made recently for a client.

The architect, Hugh Jacobsen and his family moved into it only later: therefore, and fortunately, the house is less 'designed' than it might otherwise have been.

A flexible plan oriented to the exterior was achieved: for, surprising and refreshing to find in the city is the tiny garden with flowering peach between front and street, and the garden with terrace at the rear, 3 and 5.

To the effect of the gardens must be added the effect of light: 'even on the greyest day, light and colour range from good to dazzling'. The old and new buildings are linked by a bridge above which a round bubble skylight pulls light in and down into the front hall: functioning similarly a smaller bubble is above the boys' bathroom and a light well is in the master bathroom; on the ground floor windows were built, or lengthened, to the floor. All walls are pure white.

Easy circulation around the ground floor was achieved with two means of exit/entry to every space, so that none became a corridor to another. The clear view from the dining room through the living room to the back garden, 2, and the way through living room to library, 8.

from pages 46/7

5
6 7 8

photographs Robert Lautman
copyright © by The Condé Nast Publications, Inc

The Washington home of the architect
architect Hugh Newell Jacobsen

Holiday home on St Croix, Virgin Isles
architect Hugh Newell Jacobsen

text on page 53

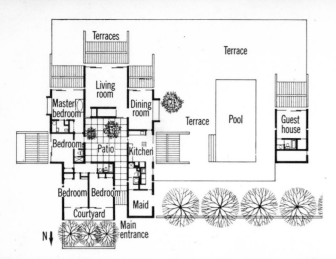

Scenically, the site for this house was idyllic but it offered challenging problems to the architect.
In solving them the form of the house took shape.
Flat roofs with deep parapets are designed to catch the rain, stored in an 85,000 gallon tank near the pool, for this is the only source of domestic water: and, because hurricanes can blow and 25-knot tradewinds are common, wind screens were necessary on all the terraces. To further deflect the air current exterior walls stand beside main walls to provide a slit between. These steeply angled exterior walls create the dramatic lines and light patterns of the structure, 4, 5.
The architect also used the house to screen from the approach side the ocean view, 4: to the right the pool and the guest house.

Only the slip of a door allows a glimpse of what is to come, 2, 3. It reveals itself as a great atrium 17 feet high and 22 feet square 'like a little town square' onto which open all the rooms including the kitchen.
The height of the structure and the open grid filter the sun, draw off from the surrounding interior spaces much of the hot air and create a breeze through the rooms even when there is none outside. Ventilation of the bedrooms can be further controlled: each has a louvered door above a solid door. The master bedroom opening to the terrace, 1, like the rest of the house, is floored with local, sealed cement tiles resembling travertine, and into it is set the sunken bath tub.

photographs Robert Lautman
copyright © by The Condé Nast Publications, Inc

Holiday home on St Croix, Virgin Isles
architect Hugh Newell Jacobsen

Two units of an apartment block dating
from the 'twenties have been internally
re-structured to form one large apartment
home high over a central area of Milan.
Accommodation now springs as two
wings from the entrance hall
(plan, page 59). To the left is
a closed, night-time area composed of
bedrooms and bathrooms; centrally the
hall flows into the drawing room, and to
the right the walls which formerly
separated dining room, study and drawing
room have been removed while the
retaining wall in the hall has been pierced
at a constant angle into a series of pillars.
They reflect the angle of the main structure,
e.g. the library storage units are set at the
same 60-degree angle to the parallel.
From the large sculpture by Moore
the obtuse angle of the central structure
permits two distinct perspectives: on one
side are the parallel channels within the
day-time area — hall, passage to dining
area, passage to study, 4; on the other,
the visual channel leading from the night-
time area, 6. One wall of this channel
slants backward, receding from the
perpendicular so that this transitional area
belongs visually to the central area from
which it springs.
Throughout the apartment white walls
and ceilings are extremely glossy
and mirror-like. Continuous steel
runners and track fitted high along the
walls bear curtains, light-sound fittings
and picture suspenders. The changing
floor levels are unified by wall-to-wall
beige carpeting — with the beige velour
upholstery of armchairs and sofas, this is a
completely neutral background to the
owner's art collection.
From the night-time area a small staircase
leads to the upper floor, a belvedere
where a continuous low window allows a
view over old city gardens, and where the
main seating is an integral bench running
along the walls, 13.
Furniture and lighting have been
designed by Gae Aulenti.

and on pages 56/61

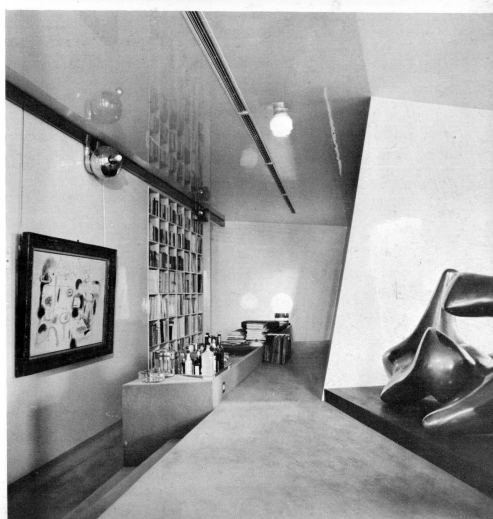

Photographs: Giorgio Casali

text on page 55

Apartment with a Belvedere for a collector of modern art
architect Gae Aulenti

Apartment with a Belvedere
for a collector of modern art
architect Gae Aulenti

and on pages 54/7, 60/1

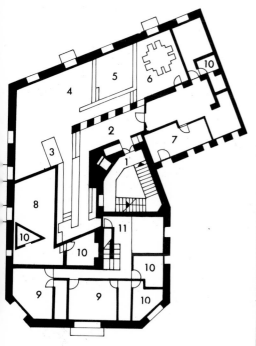

1, entrance
2, hall
3, Henry Moore sculpture
4, library area
5, study
6, dining room
7, kitchen
8, main bedroom
9, bedrooms
10, bathroom/WC
11, staircase

Apartment with a Belvedere for a collector of modern art
architect Gae Aulenti

This holiday and weekend home on Lake
Garda is set in a belt of olive trees,
cypresses and oleanders. Only its red tiled
roof is visible from the approach road.
From this close-up view on the entrance
level, 1, and the opposite more distant
view from the lakeside, 3, it is possible
to appreciate the integration of the house
into the countryside: a dimensional balance
of volume, colour and reflections always
relates to the scale of the vegetation.
The internal planning completely reverses
the traditional scheme: the main entrance
hall and the bedrooms are on the top
floor; from the hall a spiral staircase leads
to the lower floor, where the sitting, dining
and kitchen areas flow around the staircase. The arched fireplace plays a
distinctive role. To heighten the contact
with the natural setting every room has a
view over the lake, and on each floor is a
portico from which a lateral staircase leads
to the garden.
The choice of finishing materials has been
determined by ease of maintenance: for
the floors grey local stone, for the doors
plastic laminates, also grey; the walls are
simply painted white over plaster.
External walls are rendered and painted a
terra-cotta colour matching the rooftiles.

Family House on Lake Garda
architects Marco Albini and Antonio Piva

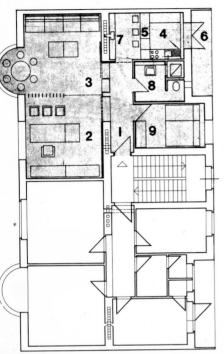

Two Apartments in Innsbruck, Austria
interior designer Egon Rainer

1, entrance, cloakroom
2, studio
3, living/dining area
4, kitchen
5, breakfast bar
6, loggia
7, heating system
8, shower, wc
9, bedroom

Photographs: Demanega

In each of these apartments, the designer has demonstrated the effect of removing unnecessary walling.

On this page is his own quite small apartment of about 80 square metres: the elimination of certain dividing walls has brought the whole into one open area within which are contained, in privacy, the bedroom and toilet facilities.

All the doors were either removed or re-positioned to maximise wall lengths or, where necessary, to screen more effectively; compare 'before' and 'after' plans. Ceiling-height sliding walls, or movable room dividers have been fitted for use when more intimate spaces are wanted.

In the larger, family, apartment, opposite, a similar approach resulted in the incorporation of the hallway into the living room. Thus a sufficient dining area and a less cramped living area as a whole has been achieved. Both apartments benefited by the entry of unhampered daylight. Both are unified and visually enlarged by all-over carpeting in a pale neutral tone. Both are studies in the use of black and white.

With the exception of the Corbusier chaise-longue all the low seating and tables in the apartments form part of a range designed by Egon Rainer and made in matt-black finished beechwood.

Designed especially by Egon Rainer, the TV mounting is incorporated in a structure designed to contain and allow to function an irremovable central heating boiler. It also contains hi-fi, and other musical recording equipment.

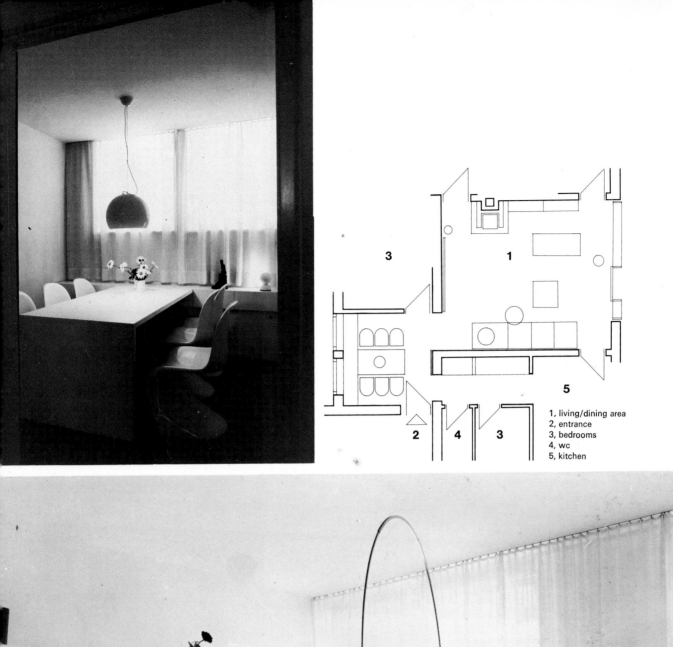

1, living/dining area
2, entrance
3, bedrooms
4, wc
5, kitchen

This family flat at Binningen, near Basle, is a changing scene of pattern and shape: a design laboratory where Verner Panton plans fittings and furniture which are later on the domestic market or are developed for special 'one-off' decorative schemes. Right, in his studio with fabrics designed for Mira-X of Suhr, and the dining room with spheres designed especially for the Restaurant Varna at Aarhus, Denmark.
Below, in the branches of the Pantower now made by Fritz Hansen Eft under the chandeliers designed for J. Luber of West Germany
Below, right, a mirror wall decoration designed and also produced in limited edition by Verner Panton
photographs Werner Neumeister

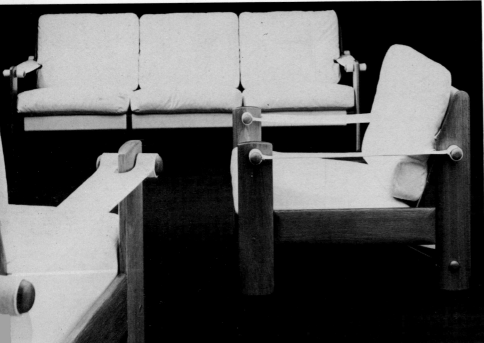

1, 2
Lompolo dining suite of stained pine
table cm 85 × 135/34 × 53 inches wide
cm 74/29 inches high
Designed by Grete Jalk *Denmark*
Mexico 2- or 3-seat sofa and armchair,
stained oak and canvas:
sofa cm 155 and 226/60 and 90 inches
wide
Designed by Esko Pajamies
All for Asko Oy *Finland*

3
Lamiline suite of 2-, 3- or 4-seat sofa,
low or high-back chairs, stool and table:
laminated beech stained natural, teak or
rosewood colours, upholstered wool or
natural hide
Designed by Sven Ivar Dysthe for
Westnofa Group *Norway*

4, 5, 6
Una casa con le tasche A home with
pockets: by means of packaged units
50² m can become a living area of 75² m.
The steps are a diaphragm, separating
livingroom/bedroom from the
kitchen/storage/service area: they provide
access to higher level seating and house
drawers, compartments for books,
utensils and other objects of everyday use.
The topmost level can be lifted to reveal
further seating or sleeping accommodation.
The single table glides on tracks through
the diaphragm from sitting area to the
lower level kitchen.
The angle of the separate seating elements
is adjustable: the elements combine into
a multiseating unit.
Designed by Luigi Massoni for Boffi *Italy*

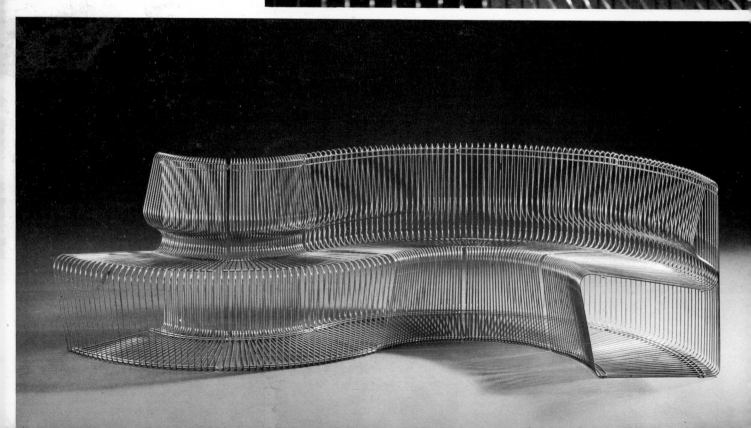

Pantonova series based on chromium-plated steel grid constructions: four basic chair shapes for straight, concave or convex seating with seat or seat-and-back cushion covered in Myralastic over form-cast plastic foam
The round table cm 120/47 inches diameter consists of six units bearing a glass top. Stools and storage units double as small tables
Designed by Verner Panton for
Fritz Hansen Møbler A/S *Denmark*

Cabinet wall, with front finish in sand velour lacquer, from a range of wall storage units in two depths and three widths: cm 40 or 61 × 38, 54 or 90/15½ or 24 inches × 15, 21 or 35 inches: also finished in white-grey or black lacquer, larch, walnut, Rio rosewood or mahogany
Designed by Walter Müller, Switzerland, in co-operation with, and for Interlübke
West Germany

Blinds and upholstery fabrics from co-ordinating designs, including carpets, made especially for Interlübke
Seating and table by COR-Sitzkomfort
West Germany

Pendant lamp designed by Verner Panton and made by Louis Poulsen *Denmark*

1, 2
Chess or drinks table *33 377*: smoked glass top covers a central hold for bottles, flowers, lighting, etc: black or white polyurethane cm 70/27½ inches square
Designed by Peter Ghyczy
Stool *11 104*: white, red or black polyurethane cm 59/23 inches high
Designed by Winifred Staeb
Chair *29 252* white, red or black cm 67/26½ inches high, moulded cushion available
Designed by Peter Ghyczy
All from the Form+Life Collection made by Reuter Produkt Design GmbH
West Germany

3, 4
Labia chair: from two injection moulded Baydur sections: white, black, brown or orange: cm 50×75/19¾×29½ inches high
Appoggio support saddle: plastic with metal base, adjustable height
Both designed by Claudio Salocchi for Sormani SpA *Italy*

5
Wardrobe for production in rigid polyurethane or vacuum-formed fibreglass reinforced plastic, dark brown or colours, cm 183/72 inches high cm 68½/27 inches square
Designed and made by David Field
England

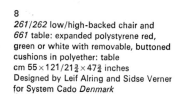

6
Occasional table of red, black or white
ABS resin: cm 70/27½ inches square
cm 30/11¾ inches high
Designed by Makoto Ookawa for
Isetan Company Limited *Japan*

7
Garden Egg: the backrest/lid, closed,
protects the Egg from weather: white,
red or yellow polyurethane shell, matching
cushions covered with Bri-Nylon about
cm 84/33 inches at widest point
Designed by Peter Ghyczy for
Reuter Produkt Design GmbH *West Germany*

8
261/262 low/high-backed chair and
661 table: expanded polystyrene red,
green or white with removable, buttoned
cushions in polyether: table
cm 55 × 121/21¾ × 47¾ inches
Designed by Leif Alring and Sidse Verner
for System Cado *Denmark*

1 2 5 6 7
3 4   8

2 4 6
8 5 7
3

1
Sofa divan-bed: soft expanded
polyurethane covered with wool jersey
A double-bed version has higher head
Designed by Carlo Bartoli

2
Talamo double-bed/day couch: the
walnut frame rests in four marble supports
Designed by Angelo Mangiarotti
Both made by Produzione Tisettanta *Italy*

3
From the *Saratoga* livingroom range:
wooden sideboard lacquered high-gloss
white polyester, with crystal shelves
Designed by Lella and Massimo Vignelli
for Poltronova SpA *Italy*

4, 5
Delfi granite or white marble table on
grooved pillars cm 180 or 220/70 or
86 inches × cm 90/35½ inches wide
Designed and made by Studio Simon *Italy*

6
Eros: from a range of marble tables
cm 70 or 40/27½ or 15¾ inches high
Designed by Angelo Mangiarotti for
Societa' Henraux *Italy*

7
Colonnata dining table: Carrara marble
or travertine: cm 120/47 inches diameter
cm 70/27 inches high
Designed by Egidio Di Rosa and
Pier Alessandro Giusti for UP & UP *Italy*

8
Green 44 range of garden furniture:
beech white-lacquered with weatherproof
static-treated polyurethane: includes
folding chair with or without arms,
cm 85/33½ inches wide, stool, folding
table and linked unit: plastic foam
cushions covered specially-designed canvas
Designed by Carlo Hauner for Bieffeci *Italy*

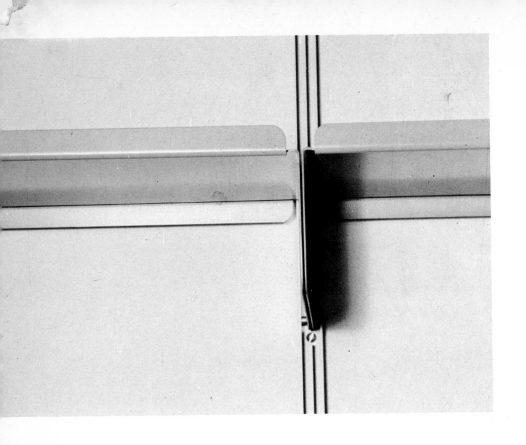

1, 2
Regalsystem 606 consists of E-profile, uprights free-standing and stressed between floor and ceiling or wall, onto which slot shelves, counters and storage cabinets: shelf surfaces veneered beech, whitewood, maple, all polyurethane-waterproofed, or grey Formica: also heavy-duty metal shelving: shelf and cabinet widths cm 65·5 or 90/25¾ or 35½ inches
Designed by Dieter Rams for Vitsoe
West Germany

3, 4
Torre, stainless steel kitchen unit incorporating sink, electric stove, chopping board, dishwasher, rubbish disposal unit The 'tower' houses a barbecue and fan exhaust equipment
Designed by Piero Batini for Eda Urbani
Italy

1
Stacking shelf units: ABS resin
yellow, red or white: each
cm 80 × 30 × 35/31½ × 12½ × 13¾ inches
Designed by Makoto Ookawa and
Sohsuke Shimazaki for Isetan Company
Limited *Japan*

2
Tyrol seat: white or orange vacuum-
formed polystyrene
Designed by Roth *Germany* for
Meurop NV/SA *Belgium*

3
Sauna stool: injection moulded
polyurethane, dark blue, dark green,
orange, yellow or brown
cm 38 × 27/15 × 10½ inches
Designed by Tammo Tarna for
Sarvis Oy *Finland*

4
Prototype table-system for rigid
polyurethane with sectional drums of
fibreglass or plywood
Designed by Jane Wright at the
Royal College of Art *England*

```
        4 7 5
      1 3   6
      2     8
```

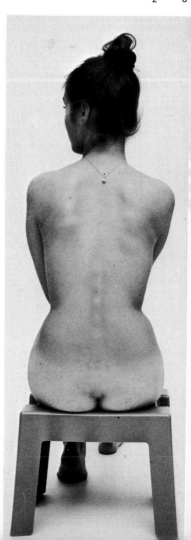

5
Castle chair: white, yellow, orange or red fibreglass cm 56/22 inches high, cm 119·5/47 inches wide
Designed by Wendell Castle for Stendig Inc *USA*

6
Esther low- or high-backed chair: polyether foam seats on white polystyrene base: upholstered in wide range of fabrics
Designed by J. P. Emonds-Alt for Meurop NV/SA *Belgium*

7
Single beds linked as pair: fibreglass white, green, red or yellow
cm 215 × 45/84 × 36 inches plus right- or left-hand ledge
Designed and made by Sopenkorpi *Finland*

8
Tomaatti lounge chair: fibreglass reinforced plastic white, red, yellow, orange or green cm 140/54¾ inches wide, cm 69·5/27½ inches high
Designed by Eero Aarnio for Asko Oy *Finland*

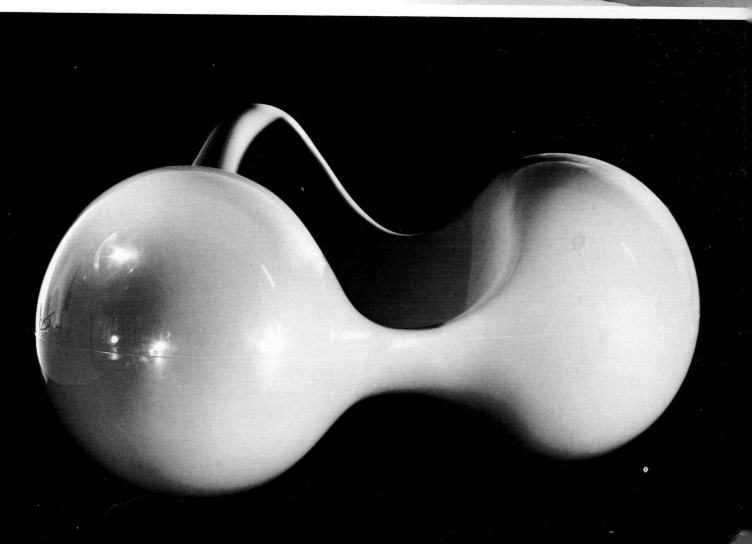

1, 3
Pillar drawers cantilevered on stainless
steel column: the drawers of preformed ash
plywood with inset line and base of red,
green, orange or yellow acrylic – the
colour a key to the drawer-depth
Designed and made by John Makepeace
England

2
Table in black beech and holly inlay about
cm 92/36 inches square
Designed and made by David Field at the
Royal College of Art *England*

4,
Child's cot/bed: converts to small bed or
full-size divan: beechwood with melamine
coated plywood panels, nylon coated
steel frames
Designed and made by Martin Fear
at the Royal College of Art *England*

5, 6
Deck bed/chair of beech with slatted
back and seat: fluted mattress covered
with deck chair canvas
Designed and made by Jane Wright
at the Royal College of Art *England*

7
Living-table or raised floor on which the
main equipment of the living room forms a
small interior of its own: rigid foam
sectioned seating covered with fabrics can
be on the table or on the 'real' floor
Designed by Antti Nurmesniemi for
Vilka Oy *Finland*

1 2 5 6
3 4   7

1
Bonanza chair: semi-rigid plastic shell
with Duraplum stratified foam 'mattress'
covered leather or weaves
Designed by Tobia Scarpa for C&B *Italy*

2, 6
Chaise Longue 248: moulded foam rubber
on steel and wood frame upholstered with
stretch fabric cm 63 × 190/24¾ × 71½ inches
overall
Chair 595: metal tube frame on cylinder
base upholstered ABS plastic
cm 86 × 85/34 × 33½ inches high
Both designed by Geoffrey D. Harcourt

3
Table 877: Nextel plastic available in
seven colours cm 50/19¾ inches square
cm 27/10½ inches high
Designed by Pierre Paulin
All made by Artifort *The Netherlands*

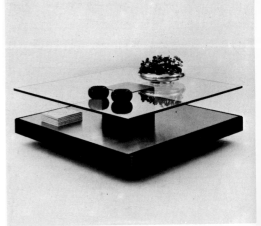

4
Ipercubo 200 armchair: weight displaces
seat/armrest in a predetermined way:
interior-sprung polyurethane and dacron,
covered leather or heavy blue denim
cm 83 × 73/32¾ × 28¾ high
Designed by De Pas, D'Urbino, Lomazzi
for Driade *Italy*

5
T147 two-tiered table: clear crystal top
centred on a cubic wooden block
lacquered black matt polyester: the lower
tier is brushed stainless steel and houses
eight drawers: cm 130/51 inches square,
cm 45/17¾ inches high
Designed by Marco Fantoni for Tecno SpA
Italy

7, 8
Pianura seating units and table: solid
structured timber with expanded
polyurethane and Dacron Fiberfil cushions
covered with weaves cm $82 \times 63/32\frac{1}{2} \times 24\frac{1}{2}$
inches
Designed by Mario Bellini for C&B *Italy*

9
Chair, pouffe and table 656/856:
polished chrome tube frame with
polyurethane foam one piece back and
seat cushion covered fabrics: the table has
smoked Perspex top
Designed by Pierre Paulin
All made by Artifort *The Netherlands*

1 6
2 4 7 8
3 5 9

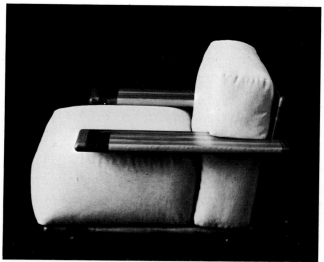

1
Single or combined seat unit: extruded
aluminium frame with cushions of latex
over pvc core, covered aniline hide:
cm 86½/34 inches square
Matching coffee or dining table with
smoked glass top, custom-made sizes
Designed by John Hardy and David Taylor
for Design Workshop *England*

2, 3
Leg-set for self-assembly of plate-glass,
slate or wood-topped table: chrome steel:
cm 46/18 inches or cm 81·5/32 inches
high
Designed and made by Atelier 'A' *France*

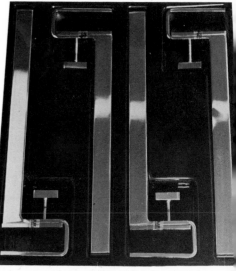

Nursery with wall storage units incorporating the revolving bed unit and built-in
chest of drawers and shelves. The front
finish is white-grey lacquer
Designed by Walter Müller, Switzerland,
in co-operation with, and for Interlübke
West Germany

1
Nuela, system of storage units: Novodur and lacquered wood components
Designed by Gianfranco Frattini for Gemini *Italy*

2, 6
S35 chair, a Bauhaus revival: chrome tube cantilevered frame: woven cane or leather seat and backrest
Designed by Marcel Breuer

S826 rocking chair: polished steel frame with upholstered body
Designed by Ulrich Böhme
Both made by Gebruder Thonet AG *West Germany*

3, 4
Chair 920: knock-down polished chrome tube and cast aluminium alloy frame: red or black hide body
Designed by Carlo Bartoli for Produzione Tisettanta *Italy*

5
From the T range: *T4* coffee table: clear or bronze glass on polished chrome knock-down frame cm 73·5/29 inches square: cm 30·5/12 inches high
Designed and made by OMK Design Ltd *England*

7
Vinda armchair: laminated oiled beech frame supports reversible cushions upholstered hide or heavy velvet: with optional neck support
Designed by Lindau & Lindekrantz for Ab Lammhults *Sweden*

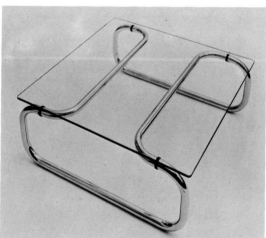

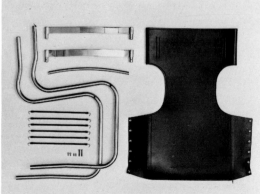

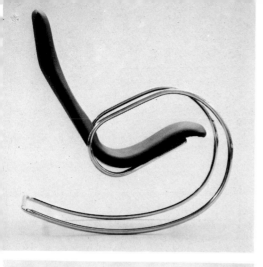

8
Jumbo Line round or square table, chairs
and shelving: polished chrome tube,
glass and leather
Designed by Luigi Massoni for
Poltrona Frau *Italy*

9, 10
WR728 occasional table: crystal glass on
Plexiglas cylinder: cm 110/43 inches
diameter, cm 35 or 42/14 or 16½ inches
high
Designed by Thilo Oerke
WR725 occasional table: crystal glass top
on chrome tube cm 100/39 inches square
cm 45/18 inches high
Designed by Gerhard Schneider
Both for Wilhelm Renz KG *West Germany*

1 2 6
    7 8
3 5 9 10
4

1
Shalimar large scale batik print on velvet:
mandarin orange, china blue or ebony
predominate m 1/39 5 inches pattern
repeat

2
Hills of Home, hand print from the
Great Colour of China range: golden
terra-cotta/caramel/grey on natural
Indian tussah. Authentic 'howdah'
upholstered windrose pink Kilkenny wool
weave with Suga silk covered cushions
All fabrics designed and made by
Jack Lenor Larsen, Inc *USA*

3
Wildlife hand screen print: project designed
and printed dark blue on white silk by
Sue Kemp at the Royal College of Art
England

1
Screen: synthetic fibre dyed in the thread
Designed and made by
Kyoto Design House *Japan*

2
Sacks K5/6 from a series handwoven in
80/21 wool/nylon on linen warp,
cm 60/24 inches square
Designed and made by Roger Oates *England*

3
Rock triptych, tied and dyed warp, plain
and patterned weft, silk and Swedish
wool: about cm 152/5 feet wide overall
Designed and made by
Ruth Ginsberg Place *USA*
collection Professor Jane Ruby

4
Floor Pad: knitted tube, stuffed and woven:
wool with polyester fibre filling: scarlet,
green, blue, purple and magenta,
cm 270/106 inches square
Designed and made by Ann Sutton *England*

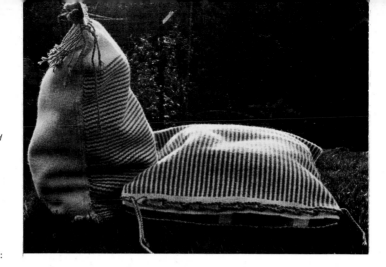

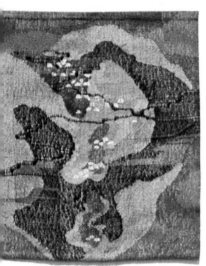

1
Ophelia washable paper from the
Palladio Nine range: pink/tan, mauves and
silver/gold
Designed by Clare Hartley Jones for
Arthur Sanderson & Son Limited *England*

2
Pueblo from the Elegant Neutral
collection of strippable wallpaper:
five colourways on lustrous foil
Designed and made by
The Winfield Design Associates, Inc *USA*

3
Chinese Peony wallcovering from the
Great Wall Coverings of China range:
five colourways
Designed and made by The Jack Denst
Designs, Inc *USA*

1
Forest: cinnamon, sand, olive or cornelian
red on natural textured cotton

2
Jester: white textured cotton with
deep brown, red, cerulean blue or
apple green, co-ordinating with matching
flax-laid, wall coverings
Both hand screen prints cm 122/48 inches
wide
Designed and made by
Tamesa Fabrics Limited *England*

3
Rhythm 'permutable' graphic,
custom-printed on fabrics or
wallcovering: here three A and three B
panels in one arrangement
Designed and made by
Elenhank Designers Inc *USA*

5
Counterpoints, HY 4642, heavy reversible
Dralon weave: three colourways
cm 153/50 inches wide
Designed by Brita Pries-Georgson
Arthur Sanderson and Sons Limited *England*

4, 6
Strome and *Cromarty* from the Island Lace
Collection: pure cotton, white, natural or
coffee cm 127/50 inches wide
Designed by Peter Simpson for
Donald Brothers Limited *Scotland*

```
      3
1 2   5
   4 6
```

1
Jezebel handprint on cotton velvet on
Mobili Tre-D sofa: brilliant clear
yellows/tea rose/lavender
Designed and made by Jack Lenor Larsen
Inc *USA*

2
Brasilia all wool rya rug: two colourways
four sizes cm 95 × 160–250 × 350
Designed by Ib Antoni for Egetaepper
Denmark

3
Ophelia 105 wallpaper: red/orange/black on
metallic gold and three other colourways
Designed by Antony Little for Osborne
& Little Ltd *England*

4
Sibelia screenprint on 60/40 linen/cotton
textured cloth: four colourways
Designed by Ulrike Rhomberg for Mech
Weberei Pausa AG *West Germany*

overleaf

1
Screenprint on 100% acrilan semi-sheer
cm 140/54 inches wide
Designed by Jukka Vesterinen for Porin
Puuvilla Oy *Finland*

2
Screenprint 9919 on polyester slub muslin:
cm 263/104 inches wide including deep
hem (width to hang): five other
colourways
Designed by Herbert Jutzi for
Ernest Schürpf & Co AG *Switzerland*

3
Terrazza designed by Peter Hall

4
Glentanna designed by Adrianne Morag
Ferguson
Both screenprints on plain white cotton,
each in four colourways, cm 122/48 inches
wide
Made by Heal Fabrics *England*

front 5, 6
Data designed by Dorothy Carr in five
colourways
Cantabrico in four colourways
Both screenprints on 100% cotton satin
cm 122/48 inches wide
Made by Textra Furnishing Fabrics Ltd
England

1
Complementary mural, curtains and carpet tiles
Designed and hand printed by
Atelier Vesna *Austria*

2
Woman batik printed wall hanging
Designed and made by Lore Heuermann
Austria

3
Model 2 printed wall hanging
cm 125 × 240
Designed and made by Karen Preben
Høyer *Denmark*

5
Flying Ducks non-repeating screen
printed and hand-sprayed panel
cm 270/3 yds deep
Designed and made by Kay Politowicz
at the Royal College of Art *England*

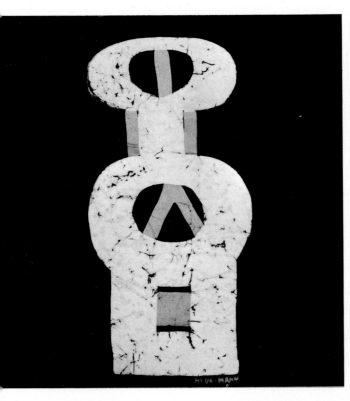

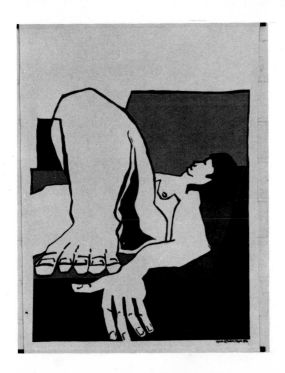

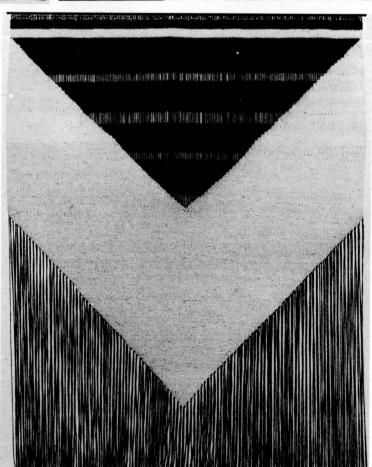

1
Camel tapestry: camel hair, red, yellow,
blue and brown wool and white cotton
cm 229/90 inches wide overall
Designed and made by Fiona Mathison
England

2
Black Flower: woollen-weave with
knotted areas of varied depths,
rose/white with black/rose centre,
m 2.90 × 5/3 × 5½ yards
Designed and made by Ruth Reitnauer
West Germany

3, 4
Two of a series of hangings of wool and
jute, double woven: black, brown and
white.
Designed and woven by Jette Nevers
Denmark

5
A Tent for Arkady: tapestry weave of
horse hair, cotton twine, carpet tape,
chair webbing, wool, cotton and other
fibres: cm 244/96 inches high
Designed and made by Maureen Hodge
Scotland

1
3 2
4

1
Bottle of manganese red, blown, glass
cm 17·5/7 inches high
Designed and made by Boris Dudchenko
USA

2
Hand blown vases in amber and opal
with fumed colours cm 17·5/7 inches high
Designed and made by Kimrie Newcomb
USA

3
Hand blown sculpture bottle in green and
red cm 12·5/5 inches tall
Designed and made by John Nygren
USA

4
Free blown form, silvered green glass
cm 30·5/12 inches high
Designed and made by Sam Herman
England

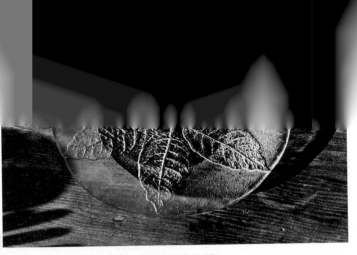

1, 2
Salad bowl and plate: clear pressed glass:
the bowl cm 23/9 inches, the plate cm 17
and 24/6¾ and 9½ inches diameter.
Designed by Ann and Göran Wärff for
Ab Kosta Glasbruk *Sweden*

3
Ducks of hand-blown glass: white with
painted decoration
Designed by Ulrica Hydman-Vallien for
Ab Boda Bruks *Sweden*

4
Marbled bowls about cm 20/8 inches
high
Designed by Heikki Orvola for
Oy Wärtsilä Ab, *Finland*

5
Decanters of clear, hand-driven glass
Designed by Bertil Vallien

6
Bowls: hand-driven clear bubbled glass
with white glass rim
Designed by Signe Persson-Melin
All made by Ab Boda Bruks *Sweden*

1, 5
Punch bowl, wine flask and glasses from
the *Capriccio 111* range
Designed by Claus J. Riedel for
Josef Riedel, Tiroler Glashütte *Austria*

2
Herzwasen heart-shaped flower bowls:
hand-made glass yellow, brown, clear or
opal cm 10, 16, 22/4, 6¼, 8¾ inches high
Designed by Sidse Werner for Kastrup og
Holmegaards Glasvaerker A/S *Denmark*

3
Rondo decanter and wine glass:
hand-blown clear glass
Designed by Ann and Göran Wärff for
Ab Kosta Glasbruk *Sweden*

4
Bowl and drinking glass from the
Mistretta 4019 range of decanter and
glasses
Designed by Giovanni Mistretta for
Josef Riedel Tiroler Glashütte *Austria*

6
Skittle bar set: carafe, shaker, ice bucket
and glasses in four sizes: handblown clear
glass
Designed by E. Kindt-Larsen for
Kastrup og Holmgaard Glasvaerker A/S
Denmark

1 4
2 3 5
6

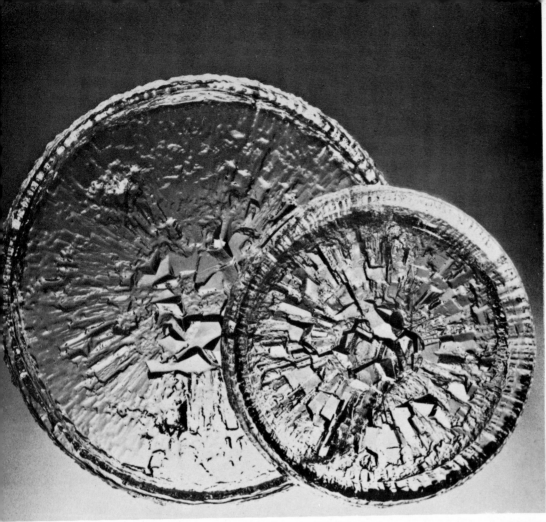

1, 2
Clear crackled plates *3449*,
cm 40 and 28/15 and 11 inches diameter
Kekkerit goblets of clear solid and
blown glass, cl 5, 11, 20, 28, 40 capacities
All designed by Timo Sarpaneva for
Iittala Glassworks *Finland*

3
Hanging plate, yellow pressed glass
about cm 18/7 inches diameter
Designed by Geoffrey P. Baxter for
Whitefriars Glass Ltd *England*

4
Grapefruit dish, heavy clear glass, ribbed
interior grips fruit, cm 11·5/4½ inches
diameter
Designed by Frank Thrower for
Dartington Glass Ltd *England*

5, 6
Square dishes, pressed and cut clear
crystal, cm 13·6/5½ inches
Fruit bowl, handblown and cut in clear
crystal, cm 12·6/5 inches diameter
Both designed by Kyoichiro Kewakami for
Hoya Glassworks Ltd *Japan*

1
Mdina glass vase, 'Ming' jar and sculpture,
silver incorporated with colours in unique
pieces; the sculpture about
cm 30/12 inches high
Designed and made by
Malta Glass Industries Ltd *Malta*

2
Pyramid of heavy Murano glass,
deep-sea-blues/greens,
cm 17 and 19/6¾ and 7½ inches high
Designed by P. Pianezzola for
Appiani Selezione *Italy*

3
Cats of handmade crystal,
cm 25 and 28/9¾ and 11 inches high
Designed and made by Daum & Cie *France*

4
Paperweight of tangerine/white cased
glass, cm 8/3¼ inches high
Designed and made by Whitefriars Glass
Ltd *England*

5
Bowls and vases: blown opal and clear
glass cm 18–30/7–12 inches high
Designed by Tapio Wirkkala for
Venini SpA *Italy*

1
Mdina glass vase, 'Ming' jar and sculpture,
silver incorporated with colours in unique
pieces; the sculpture about
cm 30/12 inches high
Designed and made by
Malta Glass Industries Ltd *Malta*

3
Cats of handmade crystal,
cm 25 and 28/9¾ and 11 inches high
Designed and made by Daum & Cie *France*

4
Paperweight of tangerine/white cased
glass, cm 8/3¼ inches high
Designed and made by Whitefriars Glass
Ltd *England*

1 2 4 5
3 6
7 8

1, 2
Paradise suite blown glasses with
contrasting textures of thin and chunky
glass
Designed by Birger Kaipiainen
Quartet tumblers, clear moulded glass
cl 15, 30, 40 capacities
Designed by Arabia/Danasco
All made by Oy Wartsila Ab Arabia
Finland

3
Azteca suite, mould-blown crystal
tumblers
Designed by Fabio Frontini for
Arnolfo di Cambio *Italy*

4, 5
Salad bowl and vases of clear glass
Designed by Olle Alberius for
Ab Orrefors Glasbruk *Sweden*

6
Ai drinking glasses
Designed by Michael Boehm for
Rosenthal AG *West Germany*

7, 8
From series 4258 full lead crystal
vases
Designed by Jan Johansson for
Ab Orrefors Glasbruk *Sweden*

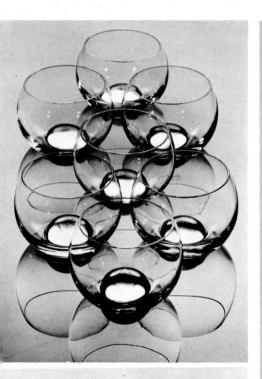

1
Napoli vases in blown lead crystal
Designed and made by Peill & Putzler
GmbH *West Germany*

2, 3
Beer glass and whisky and 'long drink'
cylindrical glasses
All designed by Roberto Sambonet for
Baccarat *France*

4
Beer glass, from the *Barbara* range of
tableware including bowls, covered
containers and condiment set
Designed by Severin Brørby for
Hadelands Glassverk *Norway*

5
Empilage suite of drinking glasses
Designed by Roberto Sambonet for
Baccarat *France*

6
From the *Romus* series: bulb-shaped wine
glasses and tall cylinder glass for
champagne, beer or vodka : fume base
ending in clear glass top.
Designed by Michael Böhm for
Rosenthal AG *West Germany*

,1   4
3 2 6
   5

1, 3
Optima, range of floor, table, and pendant lamps; aluminium painted matt white
Designed by Hans Due for
Fog & Mørup A/S *Denmark*

2
From the Mazda *Droplette* range, a triple pendant lamp: chrome or matt-black cylinders house standard lampholders
Designed and made by
Thorn Lighting Limited *England*

4
QC2 twin ceiling-mounted spotlight with two independently adjustable lamphouses: satin silver, white or brown
Designed and made by
Conelight Limited *England*

5
From the Mazda *Show-off* range of wall- or ceiling-mounted pendant lamps: spun aluminium with white, brown or orange styrene cover: about cm $16 \times 16/6\frac{1}{4} \times 6\frac{3}{4}$ inches
Designed by Alan Newark for
Thorn Lighting Limited *England*

6
Mazda *Pin-up* floor lamp: two fully adjustable reflectors slide along chrome tube on matt-black base
Designed and made by
Thorn Lighting Limited *England*

7
From the *Space Crystal* range:
clear, half-silvered or white opal glass spheres mounted on chrome tubes of varying lengths: the spheres house a 15 W or 25 W tubular bulb
Designed by Motoko Ishii for
Staff International *West Germany*

1	2	4	5
3		6	7

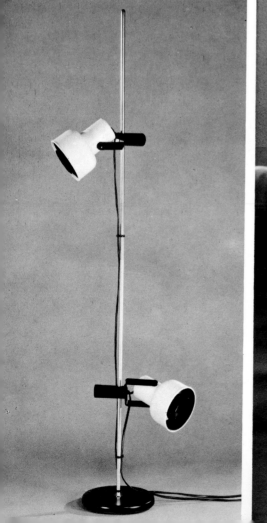

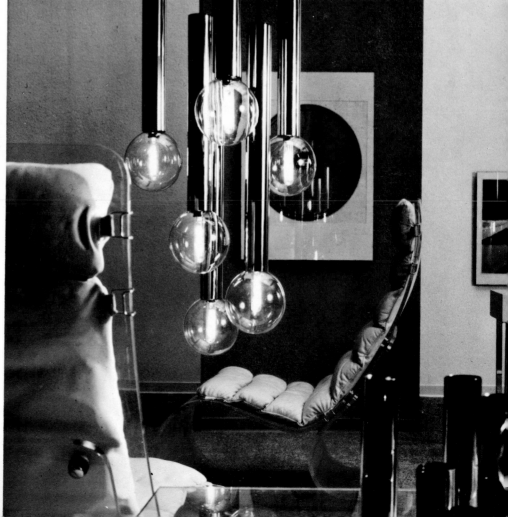

1
Pendant lamp: acrylic cylinder with
adjustable aluminium shade enamelled
white, orange, blue, green or brown,
cm 45/18 inches diameter
Designed by Jan Wickelgren for
Ab Aneta Belysning *Sweden*

2, 3
Outdoor lamps in brown rust-proof-
enamelled metal and glass
cm 35 and 54/14 and 21¼ inches diameter
Designed by Bo Anås and Jan Wickelgren
for Ab Aneta Belysning *Sweden*

4
Free-standing globe lamps for diffused
general lighting: opal Perspex
Designed and made by Banks Heeley
Plastics Ltd *England*

5
13212 from a series of rust-proofed
outdoor lamps: brown-lacquered metal
with orange, opaline or bubbled clear glass,
cm 36×39/14×15½ inches wide
Designed by Monica Strandäng for
Ab Aneta Belysning *Sweden*

6
Terrace lamps: smoke grey reflector on
opal glass pillar, with chrome fittings,
cm 68–95·5/27–37½ inches high
Designed and made by
Peill & Putzler GmbH *West Germany*

7
Membrana co-ordinated series of floor,
table and pendant lamps: handblown
glass globe with self-coloured membrane
on lacquered metal tube: opal, antique red
or green
Designed by Toni Zuccheri for Venini SpA
Italy

8
Tumbo garden lamp
Designed by Piero Menichetti for
Ismosdesign *Italy*

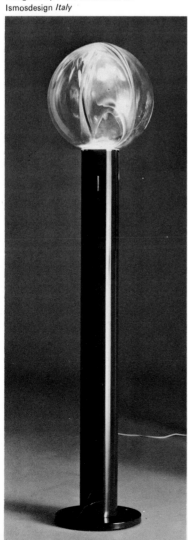

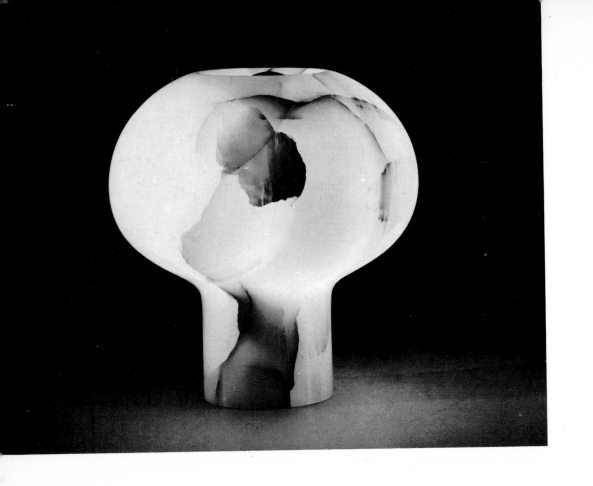

1
Onyx sculptured lamp fitted with silver
globe and integral dimming device
controlling the aquarium-like light effect
From a limited series designed by
Angelo Mangiarotti for
Iter Elettronica *Italy*

2
*The Monkey, the Bird, the Shape and
the Self,* reflected-light fittings
inspired by early mystical symbols
In wood or stone, Monkey with a brass
face
Designed by Luigi Massoni for
Iter Elettronica *Italy*

3
Il Cammino (The Road Ahead and The
Road Back) finger-tip control of the
chromium bars activates the light-cycle
from maximum intensity to darkness
Designed by Angelo Mangiarotti for
Iter Elettronica *Italy*

4, 5
Escargots floor lamp, dark amber/midnight
blue acrylic with lacquered ABS
synthetic resin, cm 40/16 inches high
Tree floor lamp, white glass,
grey lacquered base,
cm 170 and 60/66 and 24 inches high
Both designed by Naoto Yokoyama for
Joetsu Crystal Glass Co Ltd *Japan*

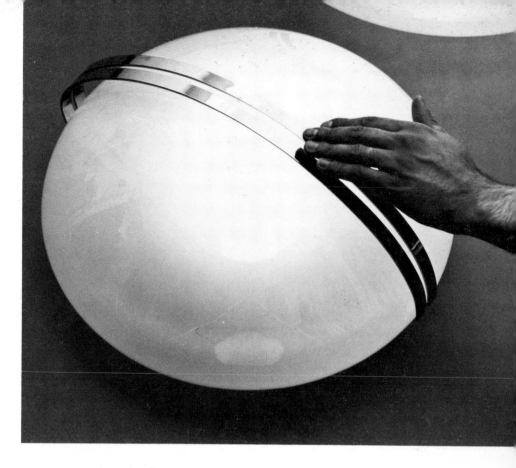

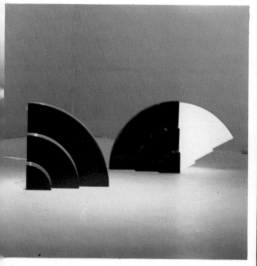

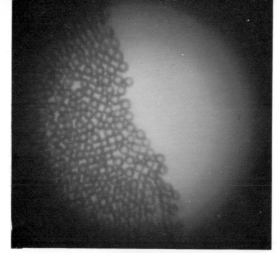

1–4
Autofade light-programme modulator in
an all-white interior furnishing scheme: the
E10000 dimmer/cycling unit used singly
or severally in conjunction with Lytespots
produces strobe-type lighting through slow
sunset/sunrise effects. Alternatively 'auto'
may be switched off and the unit used as a
conventional dimmer

5
Small tumbling glass spheres, kinetic
effect *E 10715*, one of a range available
for use with the Lumiere projector

6
Oil effect filter in Lumiere lens
All designed and made by
Concord Lighting International Limited
England

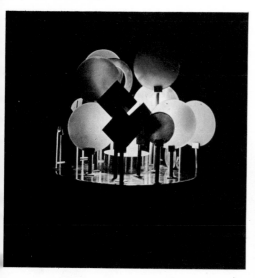

7
Custom-built table-light fitting in
coloured glass and aluminium
Designed and made by Keith Cummings
England

8
Effect-lighting fitment *6 P2*: infinitely
varied compositions result from rotation
of the screen, through which prismatic
spectrums are formed by refraction from
curved- and flat-planed surfaces
incorporated in the structure
Designed by Paolo Tilche for Sirrah *Italy*

1 2 6
3 4 5 7
      8

1
Table lamps: aluminium stove-enamelled
white, orange, yellow or black,
about cm 40/16 inches high
Designed by Per Sundstedt for
Ab Kosta Lampan *Sweden*

2
Square all-purpose Melamine containers
cm 12 or 6/4½ or 2¼ inches
From a range made by Karhumuovi for
Decembre Oy *Finland*

3, 4
Conserve, sugar or hors d'oeuvres
containers, lid operated by spoon
(detachable for cleaning)
In white, black or blue glossy Melamine,
cm 14/7½ inches high

5
Colleoni pin-box/pencil stand in glossy
white, black, yellow or blue Melamine,
cm 8/3¾ inches high
All designed by Enzo Mari for
Bruno Danese *Italy*

6
Flower and fruit containers, jig-saw-like in
red, purple, black or green Metacrilato, the
tallest cm 27/10½ inches
Designed by Team Design for Il Sestante
Italy

```
1 3 4
2   5
    6
```

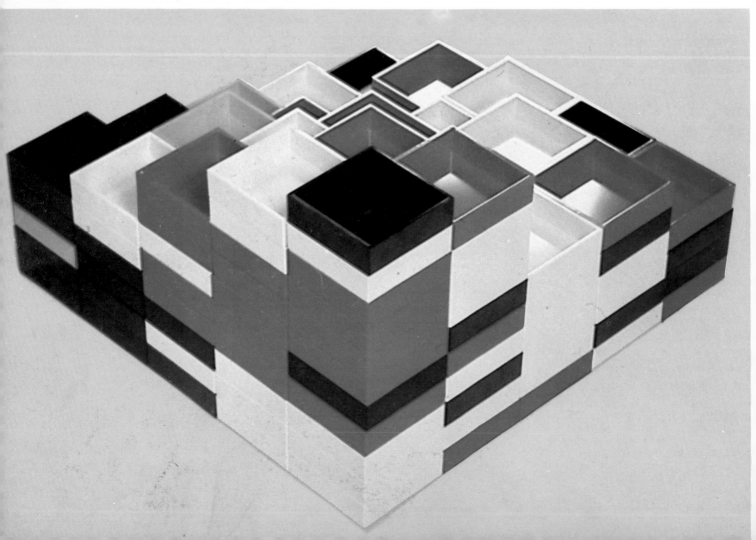

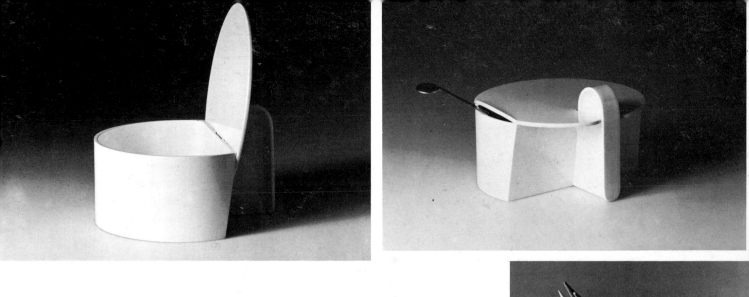

1
The Egg floor or table lamp, satin opaline glass on concealed white-lacquered steel base, cm 62/42½ inches high
Designed by Ben Swildens for
Verre Lumiere *France*

2
Pendant lamp in yellow, white or orange Astralit, cm 38/15 inches diameter
Designed by Torsten Orrling for
Scan-Light *Sweden*

3, 4
Ceiling lamp with adjustable metal shade cm 45/17½ inches diameter
Designed by Franco Albini, Franca Helg and Antonio Piva for Sirrah *Italy*

1 5
2 3 6 7
4 8

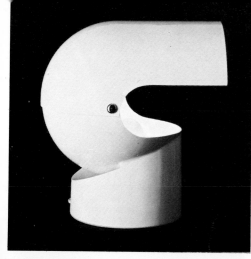

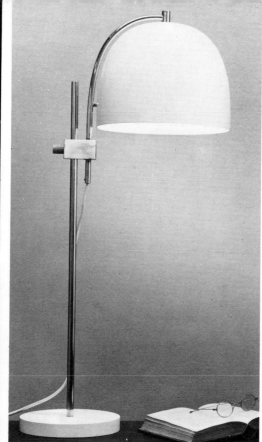

5
Mezzopileo lamp in white Makrolom
cm 45/17¾ inches high: a low,
white-lacquered metal *Pileino* and a
pillar version, *Pileo*, are available
Designed by Gae Aulenti for
Artemide *Italy*

6
Pendant lamp, grey plastic edged with
polished aluminium, cm 26/10¼ inches
diameter
Designed and made by Hans-Agne
Jakobsson *Sweden*

7
Super Egg, table lamp: chrome aluminium
stem, adjustable shade and base finished
matt white, cm 95/37¾ inches high
cm 25/10 inches diameter
Designed by Piet Hein for Lyfa *Denmark*

8
From the *Ringline* series: pendant lamps
spill lighting through a series of precision
moulded plastic rings together with full
downward illumination. White, yellow,
orange, green or purple, cm 21/8¼ inches
high. A deep drum pendant for high
mounting and a wall fitting are available
Designed by P. Boissevain for Merchant
Adventurers *England*

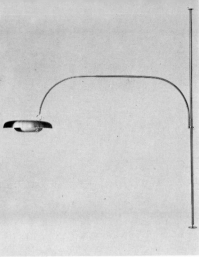

1
Modello PR fully adjustable floor-to-ceiling
lamp in spun aluminium sliding on a
steel spring-loaded rod

2, 3
AM45 pendant/wall or ceiling lamp with
swivel shade and fitting of polished metal
Both designed by Albini-Helg Piva for
Sirrah *Italy*

4
Rukh table lamp: an opal glass dome
housed in clear glass external fitting,
all on polished aluminium base,
cm 40 × 40/16 × 16 inches high
Designed by G14 Progettazione for
Gruppo Industriale Busnelli *Italy*

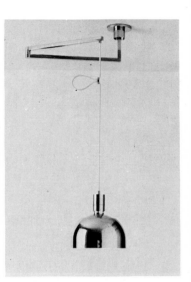

5
Floor lamp in steel lacquered white,
cm 40/16 inches diameter and
cm 143/56 inches high
Designed by James A. Howell for
George Kovacs Limited *USA*

6
Farfallone floor lamp, a vitreous-
enamelled cast-iron block from which
grows a flexible stainless steel stem
with clear bubbled glass flower head
Designed by Toni Zuccheri for
Venini SpA *Italy*

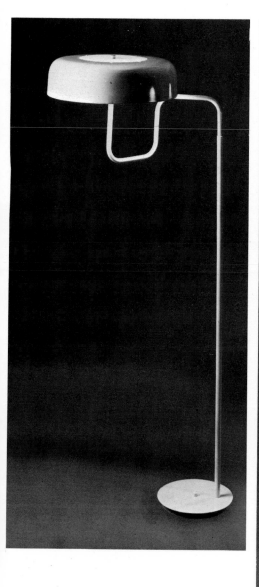

1
Pilon stackable plates of stainless steel
cm 40/16 inches diameter
Designed by Giuliana Gramigna and
Sergio Mazza for Argenteria Krupp SpA
Italy

2
Bar set in ribbed and polished silver
Designed by Massimo Vignelli for
San Lorenzo *Italy*

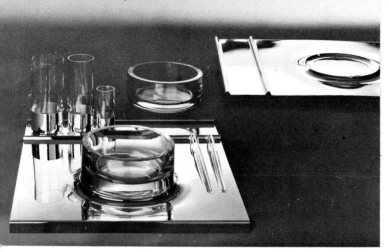

3
Place setting in heavy silver-plated
metal and crystal,
cm 35 × 39/14 × 16 inches overall
Designed by Lino Sabattini for
Argenteria Sabattini *Italy*

4
Russian tea-glass and holder, 18/8 steel,
Designed and made by Bruckmann
Bestecke Silberwaren *West Germany*

5
1000 Chromatics porcelain ware in ten
tones of gold-brown, pink-lavender or
grey-beige complemented by drinking
glasses and cutlery
Designed by Gerald Gulotta and
Jack Prince for
Porzellanfabrik Arzberg *West Germany*

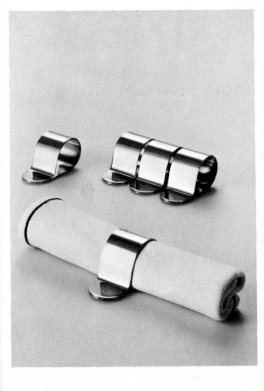

5
Ceramic fruit bowl, white, orange, grey
or yellow, cm 43/17 inches diameter
Designed by Franco Bettonica for
Gabbianelli *Italy*

6, 7
Tea/coffee set in heavy silver-plated metal
Triangular egg-holders
cm 9×9×12/3½×3½×4¾ inches
All designed by Lino Sabattini for
Argenteria Sabattini *Italy*

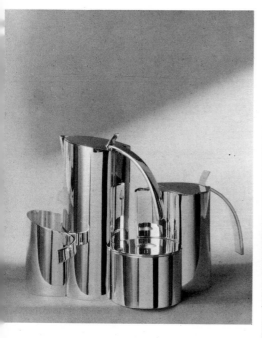

1
Table set of stoneware with hand-painted underglaze decoration: white with bands of shades of blue
Designed by Marianne Westman for
Ab Rörstrands Porslinfabriker *Sweden*

2
Casserole from the *Tree of Life* range comprising dinner, tea or coffee sets: earthenware with two-tone colour scheme: Wicklow, dark/light greens, and Kerry, amber/dark browns
Designed by Don McDonagh and
Pat McElheron for
Arklow Pottery Limited *Republic of Ireland*

3
Ts-210 fondue pot and burner of burnished stainless steel: bottom of pot is aluminium sprayed for better heat conduction
Designed by Timo Sarpaneva for
Opa Oy *Finland*

4
Emma bone china tableware: brown or
green decorations
Designed by Paul Hoff for
Ab Gustavsbergs Fabriker *Sweden*

5
Eystein range of tableware: high-fired
Feldspar porcelain with hand-painted
underglaze decoration: white background
with blue and brown bands
Designed by Eystein Sandnes for
Porsgrunds Porselaenfabrik & Egersunds
Fayancefabriks Co A/S *Norway*

6
Candleholders of black wrought iron,
hand-cut circles,
cm 9, 12 or 27/3½, 5 or 10 inches
Designed by Henrik + Jette Nevers for
Henrik Nevers *Denmark*

7
Table set of stoneware clay: brown
flowers orange-centred on mottled
grey/brown background
Designed by Gill Pemberton for
Langley Pottery *England*

1, 3
Sage and *Blue Dahlia* from the Stonehenge oven-to-tableware range: 30 shapes include dual-purpose items
Sage in green/oatmeal and maize/pale oatmeal
Blue Dahlia in deep blues on textured blue-grey ground
Designed by Roy Midwinter and Jessie Tait for the Wedgwood Group *England*

2
Provencal cutlery in stainless steel with rosewood handles and brass rivets
Designed by David Mellor for David Mellor Cutlers *England*

4, 5
Serving tool in stainless steel, cm 31/12 inches long
Marmalade pot in sterling silver, cm 9·5/4 inches diameter
Both designed by Henning Koppel for Georg Jensen Silversmithy *Denmark*

6, 7
Geometric unit dishes, stoneware glazed dark brown, cm 21×4/8½×1½ inches and cm 9×4/3½×1½ inches
Designed by Natascha Zaludová for Javurek NV *Holland*

```
                4 5
        1 2 6
        3   7
```

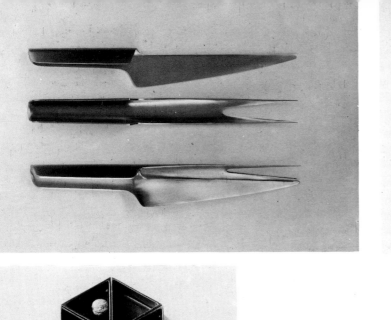

1
Voltero bowl in white, black or red marble,
or in cream, red or golden stone,
cm 30, 40 or 55/12, 16 or 22 inches
diameter
Designed by Egidio Di Rosa and Pier
Alessandro Giusti for UP & UP *Italy*

2
Split Form No 1: hand-built porcelain,
blue/green glaze, about cm 23/9 inches
diameter
Designed and made by Peter John Simpson
England

3
Group of phallic pots: hand-built stoneware, rubbed oxide decoration, about
cm 18/7 inches high
Designed and made by John Simon
at the Hornsey College of Art *England*

4
Stoneware vases, hand modelled and
glazed white/brown, brown and green
inside: cm 25–35/10–13½ inches high
Designed and made by Marjatta Lathela
Finland

5
Birds of glazed stoneware
Designed by Lisa Larson for
AB Gustavsbergs Fabriker *Sweden*

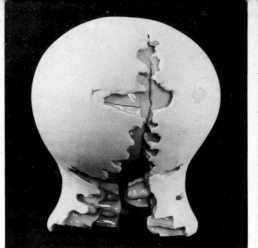

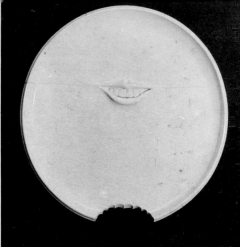

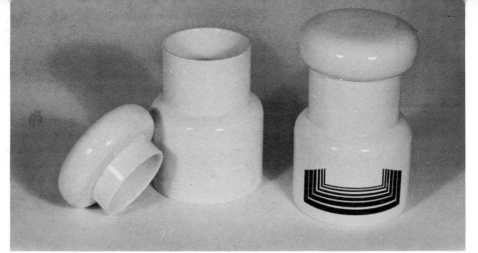

1
Head: free built white porcelain, glazed
inside unglazed outside: cm 20/8 inches
high
Designed and made by
Kurt and Gerda Spurey *Austria*

2
Mouth: slab built covered box, white
earthenware body, low fire glazes:
cm 46×15/18×6 inches
Designed and made by Vern Funk *USA*

3
Collector's Piece: thrown and cast white
earthenware tulip, black and white
butterflies, wooden box:
cm 38/15 inches square
Designed and made by Peter Thompson
England

4
Lidded pots slip-cast and clear glazed:
white earthenware, grey, black and gold
enamel transfer decoration
Designed and made by David Price *England*

5, 6
A: ceramic stoneware sculpture, painted
acrylic: cm 48×20/18×8 inches
B: ceramic stoneware sculpture, flat white
enamelled: cm 56×30/22×12 inches
Both designed and made by Myron Brody
USA

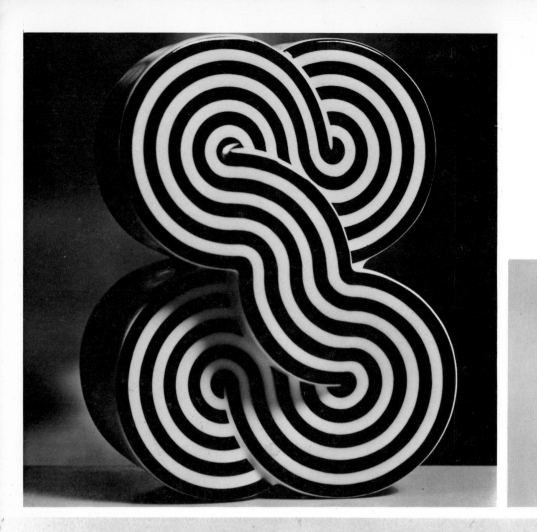

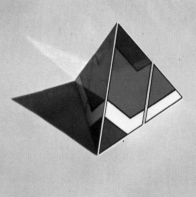

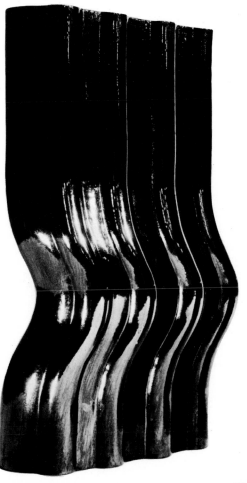

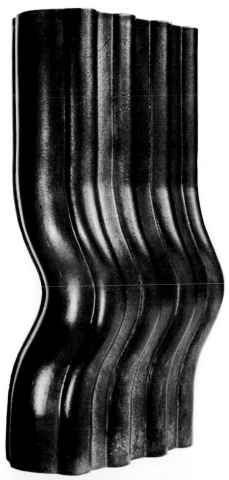

1
Object of porcelain with contrasting
colours
Designed by Natale Sapone for
Rosenthal AG *West Germany*

2, 3
Pyramid I: bone china in two pieces,
dark green, red and white,
cm 11·5/4½ inches high
Designed and made by Glenys Barton
England

4
Earthenware vases, slip cast, black glazed
with matt and shiny applied lustres,
cm 25·5/10 inches high
Designed and made by Rob Purdy *England*

5
Strips and *Curve:* floor or wall tiles which
combine in a variety of ways: twelve
colours with high or matt glazes or
non-slip finish
Designed and made by Sally Anderson
(Ceramics) Limited *England*

1, 3
Blue Bus, bluish-green glazed with
graffito pattern: cm 35×25/13½×9½ inches
wall plaque, cast fine earthenware
Resting and *Motion* earthenware dolls
with white, black, blue and green glazes
All designed by Heljä Liukko-Sundström
for Oy Wärtsilä Ab Arabia *Finland*

2
Unique stoneware: reduced fired ironglaze
in brown-grey, cm 35/13½ inches diameter
Designed by Stig Lindberg for
AB Gustavsbergs Fabriker *Sweden*

4
Composition: stoneware panel with blue
and brown glaze, cm 90/35 inches long
Designed and made by
Leszek Nowosielski *Poland*

Ceramics on pages 142 (1), 147 (3),
150/1 (1, 4), from the exhibition
International Ceramics 1972
courtesy Victoria and Albert Museum
(*Crown Copyright*):
those on pages 150/1 (2, 3), 153 (5),
154 (3), from the exhibition
Ten British Potters at the British Crafts
Centre, London
photographs Geremy Butler

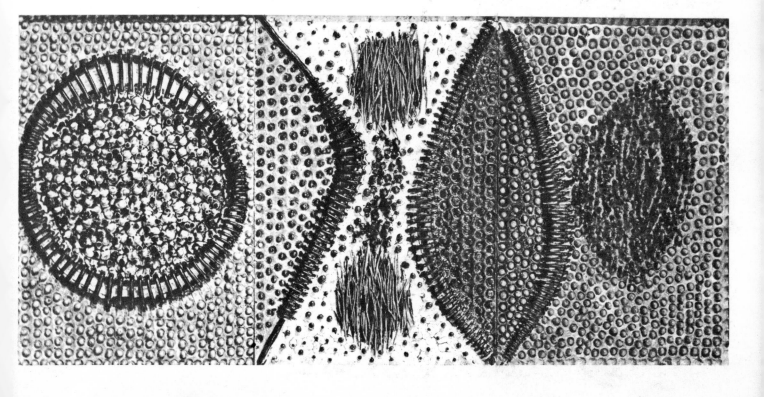

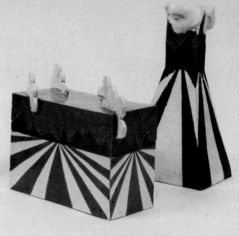

1
Vase: unglazed stoneware outside, blue
glazed inside: cm 53/21 inches high
Designed and made by
Franz Wildenhain *USA*

2
The Cook, a Self-Portrait: 26 units of
glazed white earthenware on vinyl
covered base: m 1.5 × 1.8/6 × 5 feet
Designed and made by Robert Arneson
USA

3
Cloud boxes with mysterious contents
Designed and made by Keith Booth at the
Hornsey College of Art *England*

4
Ceramic Drill: hand built, raku fired:
cm 25/10 inches overall
Designed and made by Paul Dresang *USA*

3
4 6
5 7

5
Urn: wheel thrown stoneware with cast
stoneware figurines, low fire and lustre
glazes, cm 91/36 inches high
Designed and made by Paul Donhauser
USA

6
*Landscape with car window vent and
cigarette butts:* combined wheel thrown,
slab and press-mould pieces in strong
basic colours, clay and lustre glazes,
cm 45×23×35/18×9×14 inches
Designed and made by Tom Supensky
USA

7
Slab construction, whiteware, low fire
glazes with lustres and photographic
transfer images, wooden case
Designed and made by Robb Ransom *USA*

1
Future Form: stoneware body with black,
brown and blue metallic glaze
Designed and made by Enrique Mestre
Spain

2
Object: oxidised stoneware, with gold
lustre, about cm 64 × 12·5 × 9/25 × 5 × 3½
inches
Designed and made by Tony Hepburn
England

3
Helmet: reduced stoneware with ash/clay
glaze, cm 30/12 inches high
Designed and made by Mo Jupp *England*

4
Horn Vase: slip-cast earthenware
Designed and made by Alessio Tasca *Italy*

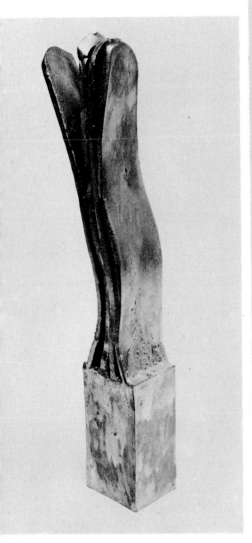

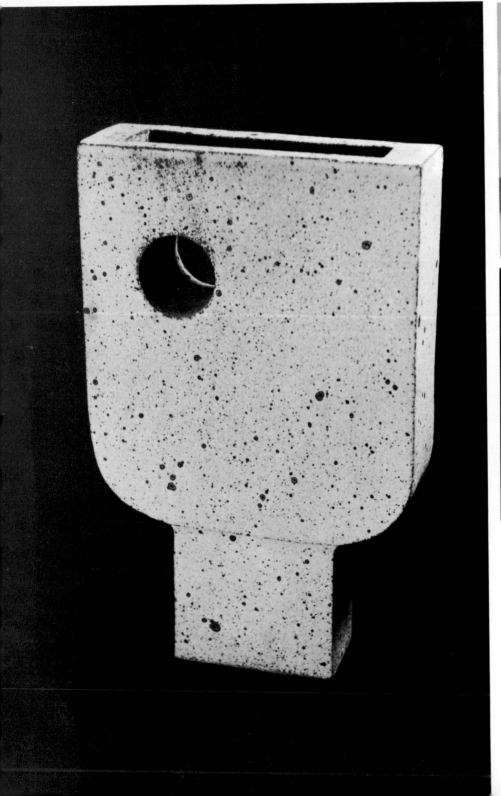

1–3
Slab built stoneware pots, one with a
very dry, high content clay glaze: the
others glazed white with rust spots and
white Dolomite glaze:
about cm 32–36/13–14½ inches high
Designed and made by Joan Hepworth
England

4
Stoneware Landscape: thrown and hand
decorated dish
Designed and made by Diana Woodcock-
Beckering *England*

5
Pot with handle of oxidised stoneware
with manganese: cm 12/5 inches high
Designed and made by Ian Godfrey
England

6
Mountain Range tea set; hand built
reduced stoneware, dry glazed
Designed and made by Sally Barber at
Camberwell School of Art *England*

1
Object: rust stoneware with thin matt glaze, cm 30/12 inches diameter
Designed and made by Eileen Lewenstein
England

2
Black bowl of pinched, slabbed and cut stoneware, raw glazed oxide and clay, cm 30/12 inches high
Designed and made by Warner Reusch
Balearic Islands
collection Henry Rothschild

3
Oval bowl of oxidised porcelain, cm 14/5½ inches high
Designed and made by Lucy Rie *England*

4, 5
Landscape Boxes: slab built stoneware with wood-ash glazes
Designed and made by Susan Wright
England
collection Reading Museum

6
Orchid holders: slip cast earthenware textured glazes: cm 20—50/8—20 inches high
Designed and made by Stephen Ainsworth *England*

7, 8
Tall square slab built boxes and press moulded spherical box: grogged stoneware body with cream and green glazes, and terracotta slip; tallest cm 69/27 inches high, spherical box about cm 23/9 inches high
Designed and made by West Marshall
England

1
2 3 4 6
5 7 8

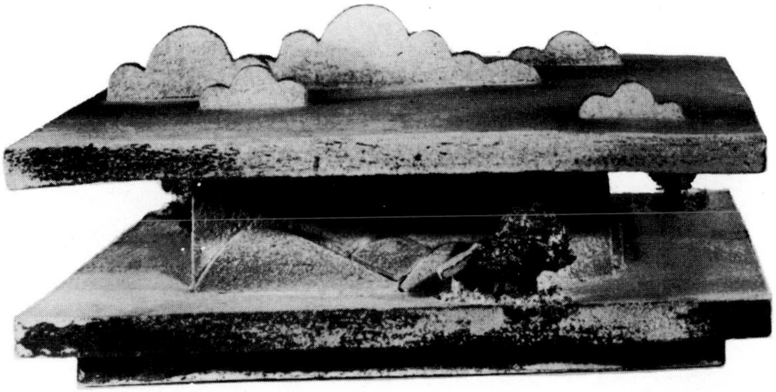

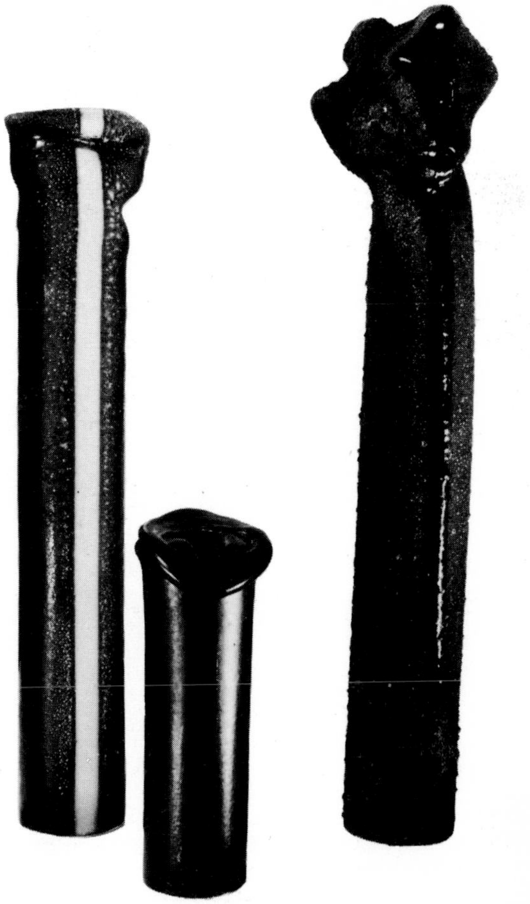

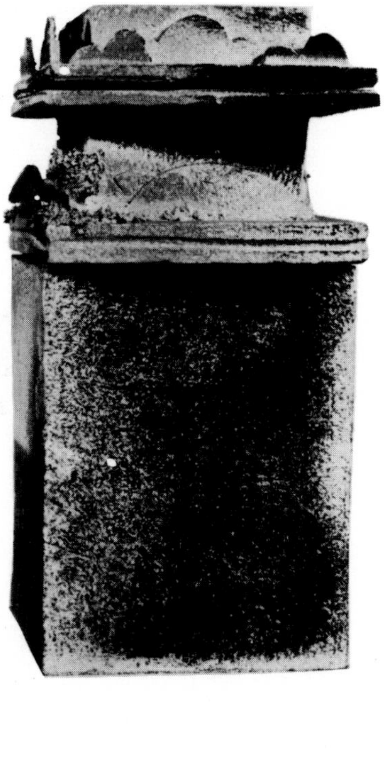

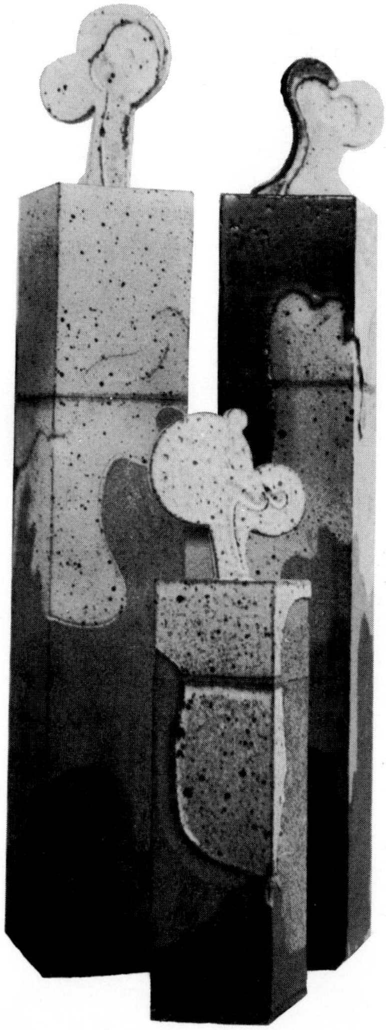

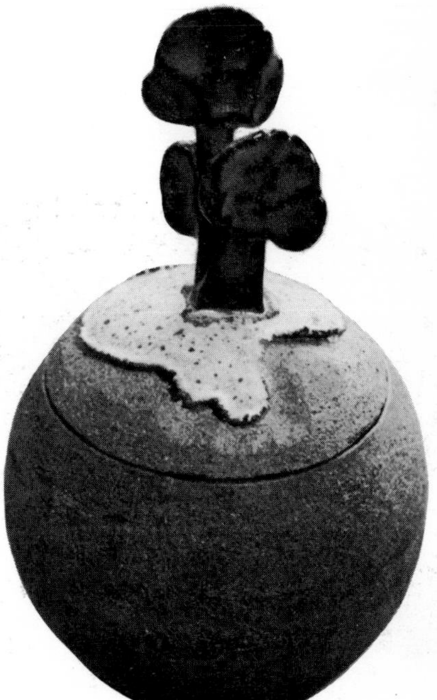

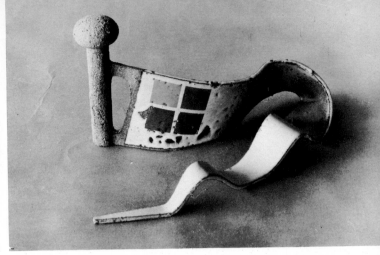

1, 2
Ceramic Flags in stoneware clay, glazed
and enamelled
cm 15 × 23–30–60/6 × 9–12–23½ inches
long
Designed and made by David Woodcock
England

3, 4
Hand: modelled stoneware, green-brown
with white cigarette, cm 80/31½ inches
high
Eye: thrown stoneware iron-flecked, light
brown-green with glass eye,
cm 28/11 inches high
Both designed and made by
Anna-Maria Osipow *Finland*

5
Unique stoneware pieces made by
Stig Lindberg for
AB Gustavsbergs Fabriker *Sweden*

6, 7, 8
Lidded pot with black decoration,
cm 11·5/4½ inches high
Porcelain slab oval vases: brown/cream
cm 19/8½ inches high
All designed and made by Janet Leach
England

Furniture

Artifort
Maastricht
St Annalaan 23
Holland

Asko Oy
Lahti
Finland

Atelier 'A'
Quip European Contemporary
Decor
226 Westbourne Grove
London W11 2RH

Bieffeci
Via V Arici 30
25010 San Polo (Brescia)
Italy

Boffi Arredamenti Cucina
SpA
Via Padre Boga 31
20031 Cesano Maderno
(Milan)

C + B Italia SpA
Strada Provinciale
22060 Novedrate (Como)

COR-Sitzkomfort
484 Rheda, Postfach
West Germany

System Cado
Finlandsgade 27–29
DK-8200, Åarhus N
Denmark

Design Workshop
Hill Top
Shelley
Huddersfield

Driade
Via Campagna 121
29100 Piacenza
Italy

Martin Fear
Willow Green
Grainbeck Lane,
Killing Wall
Harrogate,
Yorkshire

David Field
38 Palewell Park
East Sheen
London SW14

Gemini
Va Emilia Levante 295
40068 S. Lazzaro di Savena
(Bologna)
Italy

Fritz Hansen Møbler A/S
DK-3450
Allerød
Denmark

Società Henraux
55046 Querceta (Lucca)
Italy

Interlübke Möbelfabrik
4832 Wiedenbrück
Westfalen
West Germany

Isetan Company Limited
8–3 Shinjuku
Tokyo

Ab Lammhults
S-360 30 Lammhult
Sweden

John Makepeace
Farnborough Barn
Banbury
Oxfordshire

Antti Nurmesniemi
Laivanvarustajankatu 9c
Helsinki 14

OMK Furniture
14 Bruton Place
Berkeley Square
London W1X 7AA

Poltrona Frau
Viale Cesare Battisti 15
62029 Tolentino
Macerata
Italy

Poltronova SpA
Agliana (Pistoia)
Italy

Egon Rainer
Egger-Lienz-Strasse 38
6020 Innsbruck

Wilhelm Renz KG
703 Böblingen bei Stuttgart
West Germany

Reuter Produkt Design GmbH
2844 Lemförde
Hubertusstrasse 361
West Germany

Fratelli Saporiti
Via Marconi 19
21010 Besnate
Italy

Sarvis Oy
Hatanpää
Tampere
Finland

Sopenkorpi
Lahti 2
Finland

Sormani SpA
Corso di Porta Romana 82
Milan

Stendig Inc
410 East 62 Street
New York NY 10021

Simon International
Via Emilia Levaute 275
40068 San Lazzaro di
Savena (Bologna)
Italy

Tecno SpA
Via Bigli 22
Milan

Gebrüder Thonet AG
Postfach 103
3558 Frankenberg (Eder)
West Germany

Tisettanta
Via Garibaldi 129
Giussano (Milan)

UP & UP
Piazza Liberazione 52
54100 Massa
Italy

Eda Urbani
Via Teofilo Rossi 3
10123 Torino

Vilka Oy
Nastola
Finland

Vitsoe
D-6000 Frankfurt am Main
Kaiserhofstrasse 10
West Germany

Westnofa Group A/S
Ørsta
Norway

Jane Wright
38 Cleaver Street
London SE11

Prints and Weaves

The Jack Denst Design Inc
7355 South Exchange Ave
Chicago, Illinois

Donald Brothers Ltd
Dundee

Elenhank Designers Inc
347 East Burlington Street
Riverside
Illinois 60540

Ruth Ginsberg-Place
62 Rounds Street
New Bedford
Massachusetts 02740

Heal Fabrics
196 Tottenham Court Road
London W1A 1BJ

Lore Heuermann
1030 Vienna
Land-Hauptstrasse 9/29

Maureen Hodge
16 Hugh Miller Place
Edinburgh 3

Karen and Preben Høyer
Klintebjerg
5450 Otterup
Denmark

Sue Kemp
42 Dockley Road
Bermondsey
London SE16

Kyoto Design House
Oike Kamanza Nakagyoku
Kyoto

Jack Lenor Larsen Inc
41 East 11th Street
New York NY 10003

Fiona Mathison
1 Leathwaite Road
London SW11

Jette Nevers
Vaevestuen
Hasmark 5450
Otterup

Glass

Roger Oates
School Cottages
Wellington Heath
Ledbury, Hereford

Osborne & Little
62a Brompton Road
London SW3

Ray Politowicz
7 Queen's Road
Bounds Green
London N11

Porin Puuvilla Oy
Pori
Finland

Mech Weberei Pausa AG
D-7406 Mössingen bei
Tübingen
West Germany

Ruth Reitnauer
69 Heidelberg 1
Humboldtstrasse 10
West Germany

Arthur Sanderson & Sons
Berners Street
London W1A 2JE

Ernest Schürpf & Co AG
St Gallen
Switzerland

Ann Sutton
Farnborough Barn
Banbury
Oxfordshire

Tamesa Fabrics Limited
343 Kings Road
London SW3

Textra Furnishing Fabrics
5/16 Newman Street
London W1P 4ED

Atelier Vesna
Österreichisches Institut für
Formgebung
Vienna 111
Salesianergasse 1

Appiani SpA
Viale Monte Grappa 34
31100 Treviso
Italy

Compagnie de Cristallerie de
Baccarat
30bis Rue de Paradis
75020 Paris
France

Ab Boda Bruks
S-36065 Boda Glasbruk
Sweden

Cristalleria Arnolfo di
Cambio
5304 Colle Val d'Elsa
(Siena)
Italy

Dartington Glass Limited
4 Portland Road
Holland Park
London W11

Daum & Cie
Cristallerie de Nancy
32 Rue de Paradis
75020 Paris

Boris Dudchenko
Box 104 RD3
Greenburg
Pennsylvania 15601

Hadelands Glassverk
Jevnaker
Norway

Sam Herman
The Royal College of Art
Kensington Gore
London SW7

Hoya Glass Works Limited
No 1, 2-chome
Kyobashi
Chuo-ku
Tokyo

Iittala Glassworks
14500 Iittala
Finland

Kastrup & Holmegaards
Glasvaerker A/S
Norre Voldgade 12
DK-1358 Copenhagen K

Ab Kosta Glasbruk
Ab Åforsgruppen
S-360 52 Kosta
Sweden

Malta Glass Industries
Limited
Malta

Kimrie Newcomb
208 Hartle Avenue
Urbana, Illinois

John Nygren
Walnut Cove
North Carolina 27052

Ab Orrefors Glasbruk
38040 Orrefors
Sweden

Peill & Putzler Glashütten
Werke GmbH
516 Düren
West Germany

Josef Riedel Tiroler
Glashütte
Kufstein-Tirol
Austria

Rosenthal AG
8672 Selb/Bayern
Postfach 104
West Germany

Venini SpA
Fondamenta Vetrai 50
30121 Murano (Venice)
Italy

Oy Wärtsilä Ab Arabia
Hameentie 135
00560 Helsinki 56

Whitefriars Glass Limited
Tudor Road
Wealdstone
Middlesex

Lights and Tableware

Arklow Pottery Limited
Arklow, Co Wicklow
Republic of Ireland

Artemide
Via A Canova 8
Milan

Porzellanfabrik Arzberg
8594 Arzberg
Oberfranken
West Germany

Ab Aneta Belysning
Box 3067
30503 Växjo
Sweden

Banks Heeley Plastics
Sun Street
Baldock
Hertfordshire

Bruckmann & Söhne
7107 Neckarsulm
Rötelstrasse 30
West Germany

Gruppo Industriale Busnelli
Via Cialdini 137
20036 Meda (Milan)

Concord Lighting
International Limited
241 City Road
London EC1P 1ET

Keith Cummings
23 Farlands Road
Oldswinford
Stourbridge
Worcestershire

Bruno Danese
Piazza San Fedele 2
20121 Milan

Decembre Oy
Pietarinkatu 10
00140 Helsinki 14

Fog & Mørup A/S
Sydmarken 46
2860 Søborg
Copenhagen

Gabbianelli Ceramiche
11 Via S Pietro all'Orto
20121 Milan

Ab Gustavsbergs Fabriker
13400 Gustavsberg
Sweden

Ismosdesign
Casella Postale 85
51016 Montecatini Terme
(Pistoia)
Italy

Iter Elettronica
Viale della Vittoria 1534
21042 Caronno Pertusella
(Varese)
Italy

Ab Hans-Agne Jakobsson
285 01 Markaryd 1
Sweden

George Jensen
Silversmithy A/S
7 Ragnagade
DK-2100 Copenhagen

Joetsu Crystalglass Co Ltd
Gokan Tsykyono-machi
Tone-Gun
Gunma-Ken
Japan

Ab Kosta Lampan
360 52 Kosta
Sweden

George Kovacs Limited
c/o Howell Design Associates
29 Jones Street
New York NY

Krupp Metalli e
Argenteria SpA Italiana
Via Pergolesi 8/10
20124 Milan

Langley Pottery
Langley Mill
Nottingham

Ceramics

Lyfa A/S
DK-2760 Maaløv
Denmark

David Mellor Cutlers
1 Park Lane
Sheffield
England

Merchant Adventurers
231 Tottenham Court Road
London W1

Henrik Nevers
Vaevestuen
Hasmark 5450
Otterup
Denmark

Opa Oy
Fredrikinkatu 25a
00120 Helsinki 12

Peill & Putzler GmbH
516 Düren
West Germany

Porsgrunds Porselaen
Fabrik & Egersunds
Fayancefabriks Co A/S
Norway

Louis Poulsen & Co /AS
11 Nyhavn
Copenhagen K

Ab Rörstrands
Porslinfabriker
Box 100
S-531 01 Lidköping
Sweden

Argenteria Sabattini
Via Volta
22072 Bregnano (Como)
Italy

San Lorenzo
Via L A Melegari 4
20122 Milan

Scan-Light
PO Box 52
Markaryd
Sweden

Il Sestante
Via della Spiga 3
Milan

Sirrah srl
Via Callegherie 31
40026 Imola (Bologna)
Italy

Staff International
c/o BBI Lighting
Rankine Road
Daneshill Estate
Basingstoke, Hants

Staff & Schwarz GmbH
492 Lemgo 1
Postfach 760
West Germany

Thorn Lighting Limited
Thorn House
Upper St Martin's Lane
London WC2H 9ED

UP & UP
Piazza Liberazione 52
54100 Massa
Italy

Venini SpA
Fondamenta Vetrai 50
30121 Murano (Venice)

Verre Lumière
Quai National 11
92 Puteaux
France

The Wedgwood Group
34 Wigmore Street
London W1H 90F

Natascha Žaludová
Straat van Messina 29
Amstelveen
Holland

Sally Anderson
59 Little Pynchons
Harlow
Essex

Stephen Ainsworth
The Brighton Polytechnic
Grand Parade
Brighton

Robert Arneson
American Crafts Council
29 West 53rd Street
New York, NY 10019

Sally Barber
47 Herne Hill
London SE24 9QP

Glenys Barton
136 St Louis Road
West Norwood
London SE27

Keith Booth
265 Goswell Road
London EC1

Myron Brody
Avenham Apartment 8th
4132 Avenham Avenue SW
Roanoke, Virginia 24014

Paul Donhauser
Department of Art
Wisconsin State University
Oshkosh, Wisconsin 54901

Paul Dresang
Department of Art
Wisconsin State University
Oshkosh, Wisconsin 54901

Vern Funk
Department of Art
Wisconsin State University
Oshkosh, Wisconsin 54901

Ian Godfrey
265 Goswell Road
London EC1

Ab Gustavsbergs Fabriker
13400 Gustavsberg
Sweden

Tony Hepburn
10 Cecil Court
Mill Road
Leamington Spa
Warwickshire

Joan Hepworth
68 Epsom Lane South
Tadworth
Surrey

Mo Jupp
Copperville
Fawkham Green
Billet Hill
Fawkham
Kent

Janet Leach
Leach Pottery
St Ives
Cornwall

Eileen Lewenstein
5 Belsize Lane
London NW3

West Marshall
Whittington Pottery
Church Lane
Whittington
Stoke Ferry
Norfolk

Enrique Mestre
Alboraya, Valencia
Spain

Leszek Nowosielski
Podkowa Lesna
Warsaw 5
Helenowska 7
Poland

David Price
217 Weston Way
Baldock
Herts

Rob Purdy
25 Chelmsford Avenue
Grimsby
Lincolnshire

Robb Ransom
Department of Art
Wisconsin State University
Oshkosh
Wisconsin 54901

Werner Reusch
Bini Parrell
San Luis
Minorca

John N Simon
Islington Pottery
265 Goswell Road
London EC1

Peter J Simpson
Riccione
Manchester Road
Sway, Lymington
Hants

Kurt and Gerda Spurey
Schüttelstrasse 49
1020 Vienna

Tom Supensky
Towson State College
Department of Art
Baltimore
Maryland 21204

Alessio Tasca
36055 Nove (Vicenza)
Italy

Peter Thompson
8 Croft Lane
Knutsford
Cheshire

Frans Wildenhain
6 Laird Lane
Pittsford
New York 14534

Diana Woodcock-Beckerir
Glenlyn
Bare Lane
Ockbrook
Derbyshire DE7 38N

Susan Wright
153 Clapham Park Road
London SW4